Art & Design for learning

£12.99

D0245780

Children's art and the computer

KEVIN MATHIESON

Hodder & Stoughton
A MEMBER OF THE HODDER HEADLINE GROUP

British Library Cataloguing in Publication Data

Mathieson, Kevin
    Children's Art and the Computer. – (Art
    & Design for Learning Series)
    I. Title II. Series
    372.5

ISBN 0–340–57339–2

First published 1993
Impression number   10 9 8 7 6 5 4 3 2 1
Year   1998 1997 1996 1995 1994 1993

Typeset by Wearset, Boldon, Tyne and Wear
Printed in Great Britain for the educational publishing division of Hodder &
Stoughton Ltd, Mill Road, Dunton Green, Sevenoaks, Kent by Scotprint Ltd.

Contents

Series preface: Art and design for learning

Art and design for learning is a series of books which aims to provide a number of individuals involved in teaching with a platform from which to write about working with children and the thinking which lies behind their work.

The series authors are all experienced teachers and educationalists. They have had the privilege of visiting and working in schools, or working with groups of teachers who have generously given permission for their children's work, and some of their own thoughts, to be included.

In the present climate of intense curriculum development created by the introduction of the National Curriculum for England and Wales, there is a great fear amongst some teachers that room for individuality and inventiveness is in danger of being lost. If this were to be the case, it would of course be disastrous: but it need not happen.

Research historians and cooks experimenting with fifteenth- and seventeenth-century bread and cake recipes encountered failure until they realised that the key ingredient was never listed. This was because all the practitioners knew it to be such a basic necessity that everyone concerned would already know about it. The unlisted ingredient was yeast.

The same principle could be applied to many of our curriculum documents. The yeast in art and design education must surely be the life, energy and individuality of the child and the teacher working creatively with the ingredient of experience and the means. Any defined curriculum agreed upon by others and presented to an establishment, an authority, county or state is inclined to appear restrictive at first glance, especially if we personally have not been responsible for drafting it! What we are able to do with it will depend on whether we see it as a platform to work from, or a cage to be imprisoned in.

It is therefore very important to coolly appraise the nature and content of the work we are undertaking with the children in our schools and to think carefully about our personal philosophy and values. We need to identify areas of any imposed curriculum that we are in fact already covering and then consider those which call for development or may need to be introduced. It is only when we really understand the common denominator which lies behind these areas of experience that we can assimilate them into a holistic and coherent developmental pattern on which to base our strategies for practice.

In simple terms any sound curriculum pertaining to art, craft and design must surely require a broad, balanced, developmental programme which has coherence and respects the experience, strengths and weaknesses of individual children, enabling them to think, respond and act for themselves. Perhaps the real evaluation of a good teacher is to see whether children can proceed with their learning independently when he/she is no longer responsible for them.

The curriculum should make it possible to introduce children to the wonders and realities of the world in which we all live and should include art, craft and design forms from our own and other cultures and times. These can prove to be an enriching experience and can broaden the children's expectation of the nature of human response together with some experience of different ways of making art and design forms.

The curriculum should enable children to see the potential, and master the practice, of any relevant technologies: from the handling of simple hand tools to the world of information technology. It should enable them to work confidently in group and class situations as well as individually: thinking, making, appraising and modifying the work they are undertaking, negotiating skilfully with one another and discussing or talking about what they are doing, or have done. All of these aspects of education can be seen in the context of the National Curriculum which has, in the main, been based on some of the best practices and experience of work in recent years.

Intimations of the yeast component are clearly apparent in these selected extracts from *Attainment Targets and Programmes of Study for Key Stages 1 and 2*. (It is also very interesting to note the clear differences in requirements between the two stages; at seven- and at eleven-years-of-age. Stage 2 assimilates and develops Stage 1 requirements, building on them developmentally with specific additions.) At Key Stage 1 (seven-years) the operative words are:

investigating, making, observing, remembering, imagining, recording, exploring, responding, collecting, selecting, sorting, recreating, recognising, identifying, *beginning* to make connections ... [my italics].

There is a very strong emphasis throughout on *direct experience, looking at*, and *talking about*. At Key Stage 2 (eleven-years) the following expectations are added:

communicating ideas and feelings, developing ideas, experimenting [there is a subtle difference between exploration and conscious experimentation], applying knowledge, planning and making, choosing appropriate materials, adapting and modifying, comparing, looking for purposes, discussing...

What could be clearer in suggesting a lively educational experience? I believe that individuality and inventiveness are firmly based on having the right attitudes and they usually thrive best in the context of vehicles such as interest, happenings and the building up of enthusiasm and powerful motivation. The overall structure, balance and developmental nature of any sound curriculum model can allow content to flourish in lively interaction between children, teachers and the world of learning experiences.

If we persist in hardening the content of the National Curriculum in such a way that we are not able to manoeuvre or respond to the living moment, then we have ourselves forged the links of the chain which binds us.

The books in this series do not aim to be comprehensive statements about particular areas of art, craft and design experience but they are vigorous attempts to communicate something of the personal, convinced practice of a number of enthusiastic professionals. We hope that they will also offer enough information and guidance for others to use some of the approaches as springboards for their own exploration and experience in the classroom.

Preface

Children's art and the computer is a book which celebrates the fact that many teachers are now able to see computers for what they are – tools for learning, creating and designing which have their own unique functions and qualities to be harnessed by resourceful, thinking human beings.

It was not surprising that in the past, many teachers dismissed as trivia the so-called educational and creative uses of the computer, or saw them as a threat to creativity and art as well as a waste of precious time.

We have all seen a variety of programs (which enthusiasts informed us were excellent uses of this sophisticated piece of equipment) which lacked depth, quality or educational value. For example, take the program able to repeat a linear contour symmetrically – 'so useful for designing a pot' said the enthusiast, at which the teacher could be forgiven for muttering that if that was the only use that particular program could be put to, tracing paper was cheaper and equally as effective! Likewise the designs which looked like the most superficial cross-stitch, or 'binca' work, or lines 'taken for a walk' with colours which could be changed at will in the trapped shapes, which offered the children no real understanding of what was happening. So often, it seemed that the drawings we saw produced by children using computers were tight and stilted and bore no relationship to the vibrant, expressive, searching drawings we know children can undertake and which we quite rightly value so highly. All good 'hands-on experience' one might say, but what of the head and the heart?

There was a point in history when some musicians spoke dismissively of the organ as 'that box of tricks'. There is a story of an organist who responded to his recital being introduced by the words 'The organ will now play Bach's tocatta . . .' by marching up to the instrument, turning on the power, wedging a pencil under some keys and going back to his seat! I relate this story in order to draw attention to the misnomer of 'computer art'. Surely it should be termed art, where children are using the computer.

Kevin Mathieson is an art teacher who has worked in schools and in the context of inservice courses for teachers. He unashamedly approaches the computer in the same way he would a pencil, brush, or any other tool for undertaking art and design. He has found a number of like-minded teachers who are also following his approach, thereby enabling children to find their own language through open-ended, but carefully structured challenge. This leads, through exploration and experiment, to the same kind of development and skill that one would expect to see in the use of traditional tools. Kevin Mathieson and the teachers working with him would all say that there were times when the children outstripped them. Having been given their heads to experiment and find out what the instrument could do, they forged ahead and the other children as well as the teachers learned from these intrepid explorers.

There is no doubt that there are still many good teachers who feel inadequate in approaching computers in relation to art and design and it is also evident that Kevin Mathieson, with confidence in his approach and in children's creativity, is able to offer a way forward which can be based on a teacher's own fundamental beliefs and practices. In this way the computer becomes an instrument full of exciting potential: another tool for the artist to use.

In the context of the National Curriculum, possibilities for the use of the computer can be seen in all the behavioural targets outlined in the series preface to Key Stages 1 and 2. There is also potential for using computers in conjunction with direct experience or as a drawing tool after looking at particular resources. There are seldom any difficulties with children talking about what they are doing in this context or in discussion and reporting, as enthusiasm is soon built-up. I believe the work in this publication speaks for itself and shows how young children can explore, command and use tools, skills and techniques where good teaching has enabled them to experience the potential of ideas and means. The evidence contained in this book, shows that they can make personal statements and continually develop ideas.

Margaret Morgan, Art Education Consultant

Acknowledgments

I would like to say a very special 'thanks' to Julia whose contribution to this book is immeasurable. I would also like to thank the following teachers and headteachers for allowing me to work in their schools and to reproduce the work I have done with them and their pupils:

Julia Holland, Carmel Moore, Gwenda Smale, Catherine Sinclair, Jan Hughes, Val Turner, Colin Roker, Anna Williams, Ken Winger, Joanne Masters and Karen Hunter.

I would also like to thank the children and teachers of those Enfield schools whose work is reproduced in this book:

Prince of Wales Primary; Bowes Primary; Winchmore Junior; Latymer All Saints and Eversley Infants.

Thanks too, to Neil Turner of Glenwood School, Bedfordshire, for the examples of work by children with severe learning difficulties.

I would also like to thank Peter Evans, Keith Butcher and Marianne Scheer who together make-up the Enfield IT team, for their on going support and Margaret Morgan for her constant encouragement, advice and ideas throughout this project. Lastly I would like to thank everyone who has helped by contributing thoughts and ideas during the process of writing this book.

All the works reproduced in this book were produced on a Standard Acorn Archimedes A 3000 computer using Pro-Artisan and Flare software and printed out via an Integrex Colourjet 132 Printer.

The cover artwork was produced by Beverley Russel of Prince of Wales Primary School and is based on Henri Rousseau's *Tropical Storm with a Tiger ('Surpris!')*.

Thank you to the British Museum in London for the use of figure 1 a section of Charles Babbage's 'Difference Engine' (negative number b/w 26592) and the National Gallery, London, for permission to reproduce *Tropical Storm with a Tiger ('Surpris!')*.

This book is dedicated to Eleanor, Richard, Jessica, Gary, Andrew and all the children I have worked with, in gratitude for the enormous pleasure that their work has given me and others.

The historical context of the computer

Historically, artists have always sought to use new materials to express their ideas, views and feelings about the world around them. From the beginning of mankind's history when the first cave paintings were produced, individuals have used whatever materials were readily available to them for art, such as earth, berries and burnt wood. Since then there have been many movements in art which have sought to challenge what went before and use new materials and processes.

It is clear that particular methods of working and specific techniques were developed by different people in various places to suit their own individual needs and priorities. However, the common thread which underlies all development is a combination of an understanding of the environment, a knowledge of available tools and materials, an understanding of scientific and mathematical advances, curiosity and the desire to create.

Freedom to express ideas and philosophies and to explore the nature of materials now seems commonplace to us. To work in two- or three-dimensions, to record on film and video or to work on a computer, form part of our choice of media, in fact we are confronted by this technology in our own homes every day. Yet in relation to the traditional arts, computers have a very short history. The development of modern desktop computers, however, has its foundation in a traditional craft medium.

The term computer as we use it now refers to a machine. It is therefore difficult for us to comprehend that in the nineteenth century the term 'computer' was used by Charles Babbage, an ancestral figure in British computing, to describe people who performed calculations. There are similar examples of people being described as computers as late as the 1950s, and it was around this time that the term 'computer' was applied to a new machine – the electronic computer.

These first computers could not be bought by individuals and were to be found only in universities, military establishments or industry and, despite their size, they were not very powerful. By the mid-1970s computers had taken their place alongside televisions and hi-fi systems in our high street stores.

The earliest tools used to assist us in problem solving were counting machines, the Chinese abacus probably being the best-known example. By moving the beads in a certain order, calculations could be made. In the seventeenth century attempts were made to devise a mechanical tool which would add and multiply. These early attempts were unsuccessful due to the fact that they could not carry numbers to the next column. It wasn't until the nineteenth century that these problems were solved, when, in 1834, the Swedish father and son team of George and Edward Scheutz were the first to construct a machine or Difference Engine as it was called, which calculated tables automatically.

In England, Charles Babbage, the brilliant mathematician designed a Difference Engine which, sadly, was never completed due to continuous financial difficulties. Babbage's design was partly modelled on designs and images from the textile industry. Despite being disappointed at this failure he went on to design a totally new

Figure 1   A section of Charles Babbage's Difference Engine – reproduced with permission of the Science Museum, London

kind of machine which he called the Analytical Engine, and in doing so made a giant leap forward.

Unlike the Difference Engine (see figure 1) which could only calculate fixed, simple mathematical operations, Babbage's Analytical Engine was to be a programmable machine which could calculate almost any algebraic equation. This machine shared many of the features which we find in modern computers and remains one of the major achievements of the nineteenth century.

The machinery which did the calculating was called the 'mill' (processor). This was kept separate from the columns of numbered cogs which represented the 'store' (memory).

The designers of modern computers arrived at a similar arrangement without knowledge of Babbage's designs. The other significant breakthrough for Babbage was that his machine was programmable: the instructions would be stored on punch cards as were the instructions for early computers. The punch card idea came from the Jacquard loom which used cards to control patterns woven with thread. Ada Lovelace, a mathematician and friend of Babbage, wrote the following to describe the new machine: 'It weaves algebraic patterns just as the loom weaves flowers and leaves.' (Palfreman and Doron, 1991).

It took another seventy years for Babbage's concepts to be implemented when in 1944 the world's first programmable computer, the Mark 1, was completed by Howard Aitken of Harvard University and IBM. Eighteen years later Ivan Sutherland, a young graduate at Massachusetts University, demonstrated a program called sketchpad. Sutherland used a light pen to draw circles of different sizes on a small screen and was able to cut them out and paste them in just the same way as we might do on a modern computer drawing package. The first graphics program had been invented and it offered a glimpse of what modern computers would become.

1 Computers in the primary classroom

THE EARLY STAGES

I am an art teacher who recognised early on in my own computer experience the rich potential that computers offered for creative work. However, at the same time, I also feared that the computer programs which I saw then, might well stifle the creativity which I perceive to be the real value of art and design education.

Initially I experimented on computers which today look very old fashioned. I typed in short programs which, when run, drew a simple picture on the screen. The kind of images which could be produced were very similar to Teletext pictures and even though colour monitors were available, colour printers were rare. I was aware that more powerful computers existed and that these machines offered many more creative possibilities but the price of them was beyond the reach of the average school or individual.

I continued to maintain my personal interest in new technology and as new computers arrived at the school in which I worked, I would buy or borrow art programs and experiment. I spent many lunch-times and evenings exploring different ideas and looking for ways in which I could incorporate computer art into my teaching. It would often take hours to do a drawing or to produce a repeat pattern for textiles but I persisted spurred on by the knowledge that computers should be able to assist the design process as this was already happening in design studios. As an art teacher I saw the potential! However, on the other hand, I could not justify children spending many hours on a computer creating images which could have been produced in minutes with a stencil and some coloured pencils.

On reflection what I was doing was building up my own expertise but I had many reservations about using this expertise in the classroom. I could not expect my colleagues and the children I was working with to go through the same processes that I had been through. An added problem was that the technology was changing rapidly. New programs promising more flexibility became available

14

but were often complex and difficult to use because they were trying to imitate the kinds of processes available on more powerful computers. It was difficult therefore to find a meaningful starting point from which children could launch their experimentation and achieve something creatively worthwhile.

THE FIRST BREAKTHROUGH

Fortunately for all of us, the new generation of school computers are, to use the jargon, 'user friendly'. If you have used one you might at times think they were designed to be the opposite; nevertheless, they are more sophisticated than their predecessors and the programs which are available, offer real possibilities for creative work.

Through working with primary and secondary teachers and working experimentally with children, I came to realise that the computer is no more or less than a tool. It offers a range of possibilities and can be approached in as basic a way as any other graphic tool such as pencils, paint, or printmaking tools. Computers should certainly not be feared for they can offer different but supportive experience to the basic range of two- and three-dimensional art and design which is offered in schools.

I have always believed that one of the most effective ways for children to learn is by experimentation and research. This is strengthened when a teacher has a deep interest and understanding of the ways in which young children develop and learn. When dealing with drawing, colour, form, materials and media it was a natural thing for us as teachers to encourage the children to experiment in order to find out what could be achieved and I approached the computer in the same way. The children were far more confident in their experiments than the adults I worked with and often broke new ground. The really exciting thing was that the imagery which was the outcome of this approach was akin to the best of their experiments with other media rather than the stilted games and restricted end-products which were the results of closed-ended computer challenges. Once children began to work on an open-ended art program they started to recognise the possibilities open to them. Changing colours for example, instantly changed the mood and feel of an image.

Figure 2   Children working in a pair on the computer

Computer art and design is part of the broad field of experience which we should be offering children and we should see it as both a means to an end and, sometimes, as an end in itself. What is clear is that it can never take the place of the basic tools and materials – in fact, for a few children, it may even be a barrier between themselves and direct creativity but, for most, it offers another means of expression, communication and learning. In some cases computer art can be a breakthrough which is particularly appropriate for children with learning or behavioural difficulties, or physical disabilities. (Sometimes providing the opportunity for such a breakthrough to occur requires the provision of special equipment, see figure 3 below.)

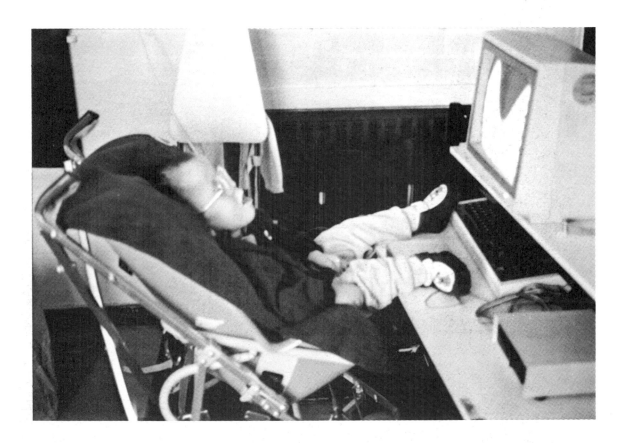

Figure 3   A child with physical and mental learning difficulties controlling a cause and effect program with his feet, via a block switch using a shape program. The stimulus is both visual and auditory. In some cases the access to the experience is more important than the outcome

Most children possess a natural curiosity, a willingness to learn and a desire to investigate and the computer usually triggers these natural responses. I have worked with children aged between four- and eleven-years using art programs. These programs are designed in such a way as to imitate an art room in electronic form. Children can take charge of this environment and in doing so feel a sense of achievement. This is because the feedback is immediate and children can assess, adapt and develop their own work through the process.

Figure 4   An exciting first image produced by a five-year-old

The interactive nature of Information Technology (IT) can lead to teamwork and co-operation amongst pupils and teachers and various levels of discussion can ensue. Verbal skills (as well as traditional art skills) are required when children are engaged in the designing process as it involves defining problems, seeking strategies and testing results. An example of this was a task to design information signs for use around the school. First the children had to identify what signs were necessary, for example: No running. Keep to the left. Dining area. They then designed the signs working in groups and chose different shapes and colours depending on the kind of information which was to be included. They then tried using different backgrounds and lettering. Each group presented their sign to the rest of the class and the work was discussed. The image on the computer screen was the focus of the discussions and the chosen signs were then printed out. The different signs were placed around the school and a survey was carried out to find out which signs communicated the information most effectively.

This activity was part of a project on signs and symbols and involved problem solving in which the problems and solutions were identified, tested, evaluated and then improved upon. In this context learning becomes understanding rather than a set of right answers and children who use computers in this way often approach problems in other areas with greater confidence. It was also often surprising and a great pleasure to note how intensely the children worked. Many were able to be fully involved in deep concentration for long periods of time.

I also found that working with computers in the classroom gave opportunities for children and teachers to explore possibilities together in joint learning experiences. Some of the children in the groups were less confident than others but they worked together and I ensured that everyone was challenged and experienced success at every stage, this in turn built-up their self-confidence.

TEACHING AND LEARNING EFFECTIVELY — FINDING THE RIGHT APPROACH

As a teacher I know that effective learning takes place when children are actively involved in purposeful activities which hold interest and meaning for them. My aim is for children to be so motivated that they will continue to develop progressively and hopefully leave the education system with the ability to go on and learn throughout their lives.

In my own teaching and when working with colleagues in primary and secondary schools and teacher training institutions I maintain that it is important to consider the physical environment which children inhabit as they learn, as well as the tools, materials and resources which they use. Stimulation is very important as is the whole ambience of the learning environment and an atmosphere which promotes respect and an ability to work with others. The school environment should be conducive to work in and above all interesting.

Similarly, whatever we challenge children to do must be equally as well ordered and stimulating and must be seen as part of a developmental sequence with each child unfolding and learning. Our skills should be directed towards offering children appropriate challenges which build on what has gone before and lead on to the next stage. In discussion with teachers at the schools in which I have worked on computer art we aimed to find targets which were meaningful and then we discussed and negotiated some of these with the children.

For such active learning pupils need to participate in learning situations which matter to them, for it is by capturing their attention, interest and imagination that they become willing to accept the challenge of the experience and begin to use their own initiative. Getting children to ask themselves the question 'Where can we go from here?' rather than waiting for the teacher to define the next step for them, required constant encouragement.

I aimed to communicate clearly and effectively and to encourage children to discuss new ideas and to try out new approaches and concepts. I feel, however, that it is important to provide a wide range of learning opportunities which should be valued and celebrated by the school community. I believe this to be the best kind of educational learning and the most effective approach to children's art and computers.

HOW TO BEGIN – THE NEED TO EXPERIMENT

Most primary, special and middle schools now have several computers. In the past the responsibility for the computer was often given to a mathematics teacher and the programs which were used were limited to disciplines other than art and design and, in the first instance, offered little opportunity for interaction between disciplines or for creativity. Now the number of computers in schools is increasing and the quality and range of both hardware and software has extended.

Whether we are experienced, having undertaken inservice training, or whether we have little experience to date, there is a rich potential for creative teaching and learning through computers. With the same basic tools and the same basic techniques either simple or sophisticated imagery can be created just as with the pencil or paintbrush. There are still, however, many excellent teachers who lack confidence in this curriculum area, together with others who are, at times, inclined to see this wonderful tool as an end in itself rather than another rich means for learning, experimentation, research, communication, design, and expression.

In order to facilitate learning on the computer you do not have to be an expert. Each piece of software has many features but you don't have to be familiar with everything: start small and move on to other areas when you feel more confident. Be willing to experiment! Children should be guided through a series of processes where skills can be developed and applied to activities in a progressive and sequential way. Using this approach the computer becomes a useful tool rather than being just a novelty or toy which has limited value.

It is very important to have clear aims before embarking on computer work or the danger is that the nature of the program dictates the outcome of the learning experience. The challenges set need to be appropriate to the learning programme which is undertaken. In this context children and teachers can explore possibilities together thus providing a stimulating learning experience.

This book aims to draw together many elements of good practice in order to develop a rationale for using computers as part of a developmental learning programme within art and design education, for, as Joan Scott suggests in the following extract, few inventions this century have made such a big impact on our lives or have changed the world as fundamentally as the computer.

> Nothing in the last half century has affected our lives and the world we live in more than two inventions, the television and the computer. Computer graphics is the artful and scientific fusion of these two and a prism refracting new visions of the earth, our lives, our inventions, our imaginations. It is the image of the future today.
> (Joan Scott, 1984.)

2 Understanding the computer

In order to facilitate the learning of computer art, teachers need to have a basic understanding of computers. In this chapter I will outline what computer hardware and software are and the functions and key tools on offer in most art programs, before going on to discuss IT capability and the role of IT with art. I stress again, we do not need to be experts but a grasp of the following fundamentals would be helpful.

WHAT IS A COMPUTER?

A computer system is a collection of different components which work together. The following section describes the various components.

Hardware

Hardware is the term used to describe the computer (or processor), a floppy disc drive, input devices (usually a keyboard or mouse), output devices (a monitor or screen) and a printer. Collectively this is called the computer system. (See figure 5.)

Figure 5
A computer system

- The computer (or processor) – this is the brains of the system containing the microchips which process the information.
- Floppy disc drive – most computer systems come supplied with a disc drive. It is used both to load the software which provides information to run the system and as a means of storing and reloading work. 5.25" or 3.5" disc drives are available.
- Input devices – the keyboard and mouse are the most commonly used input devices and are supplied with the system. The keyboard is used for entering commands and data. For art purposes the mouse is the most common input device. It is a tool used to control what is happening on the computer screen. However other input devices which serve the same purpose are available and some users may find them preferable.

1 *Trackerball* – this is a ball mounted in a block. When the ball is rotated the cursor or pointer moves on the screen.

2 *Graphics tablet* – this is composed of a flat drawing surface and a pen or stylus either attached or unattached. Pictures can be created by moving the pen across the drawing surface and pressing lightly.

3 *Light pen* – this is a pen which is sensitive to the light from the computer screen. The pen will have a small switch, and when moved over the screen will draw.

4 *Touch screen* – this is a device which can sense what part of the screen has been touched. Items from the screen can be chosen by pointing.

5 *Cordless mouse* – this is a mouse without a tail or wire connecting it to the computer. This type of mouse operates in a similar way to a television remote control. Items can be selected from the screen providing the mouse is in line with the sensor.

6   *Video digitiser* – this is an electronic board connected to the computer which allows still images to be captured from either a video recorder or a video camera. The images can then be combined with drawn art work.

7   *Scanner* – this is an input device which enables text or graphic images from paper originals to be loaded into the computer.

In choosing any input devices you should consider the needs of the children you will be working with and always avoid buying new equipment without first seeing it to assess its capabilities. Some children may take readily to any input device; others will need additional support in finding the most appropriate to suit their needs.

• Output devices – a screen is the most common output device. It provides a window on to the computer environment. The printer is used to gain a printout or 'hard copy' of the screen image.

Criteria for choosing hardware

As individuals we often have little choice in deciding which computer system our school buys as this depends on LEA and school policies and, of course, on cost. In addition to this the choice is dictated by the availability and suitability of programs which can be used across the curriculum. However, it should be remembered that whatever computer system is chosen the skills acquired by your pupils will be transferable to other systems.

Software

The software drives the hardware of the computer by telling it what to do. Software is 'soft' because it is easily changed without affecting the hard wired circuits of the computer. It is loaded into the computer via the disc drive. 'Paint or draw software' is a collective name given to the basic software which is used in art and design and there are many packages which are commercially available to choose from. All the children's work shown in this book was carried out on paint software.

I have no intention of recommending particular pieces of hardware or software as the processes I describe can be carried out on many different computers with different makes of software. However, it would be fair to say that in the field of art software, the tools and features available are now fairly standard and any variations which do exist are simply differences dictated by the hardware in use. However, software which has been written for one make of computer will not necessarily run on another make of computer. This is because each type of computer has its own particular operating system. From this point in the book I will refer to the software as the program or art program as this is the term I have most often encountered in schools.

We often hear the term 'user friendly' when we talk about modern computers. The words are used to describe the computer environment which we are working in. Most computers now run on what is called a WIMP system (windows, icons, menus and pointers).

- A window – is an active area of the computer screen.
- Icons – are small pictures representing programs, tools, files and options.
- The menus – are lists of options on offer.
- The pointer – is a floating arrow which moves across the screen as the mouse is moved on a flat surface. Different tools or facilities can be selected by clicking the mouse.

This system of selecting items from the screen by using the mouse and pointer speeds up our ability to access the various parts of the program and with only a small amount of practice we can become quite skilled. This way of working also minimises the need to use the keyboard although the exception is when we are working with text or need to 'save' our designs, that is, place them permanently or semi-permanently on disc.

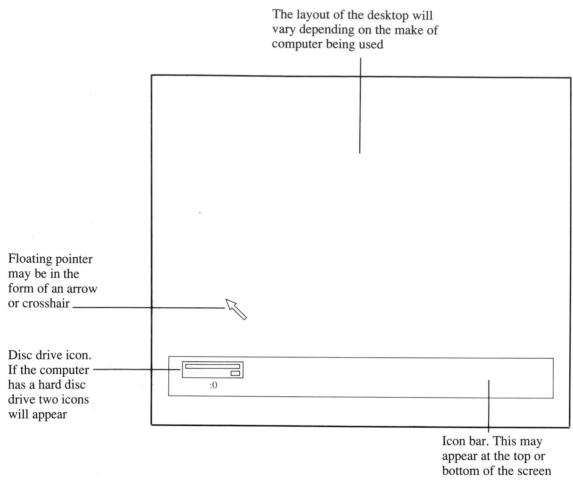

The layout of the desktop will
vary depending on the make of
computer being used

Floating pointer
may be in the
form of an arrow
or crosshair

Disc drive icon.
If the computer
has a hard disc
drive two icons
will appear

:0

Icon bar. This may
appear at the top or
bottom of the screen

Figure 6   A basic desktop

It may be useful to think of the computer as your workplace.
When we arrive and switch on we are presented with a desktop. (See
figure 6 above.) In its simplest form the desktop is often a coloured
strip at the top or bottom of the screen which shows the make of the
computer and an icon representing the disc drive. The software is
loaded by inserting the disc into the disc drive and then clicking on
the disc icon with the pointer. This activates the drive loading the
information from the disc into the memory of the computer. Once
loaded you are presented with a window displaying a number of
icons. Clicking on the program icon makes the drawing area and
tools appear. (See figure 7 opposite.) Somewhere on the screen there

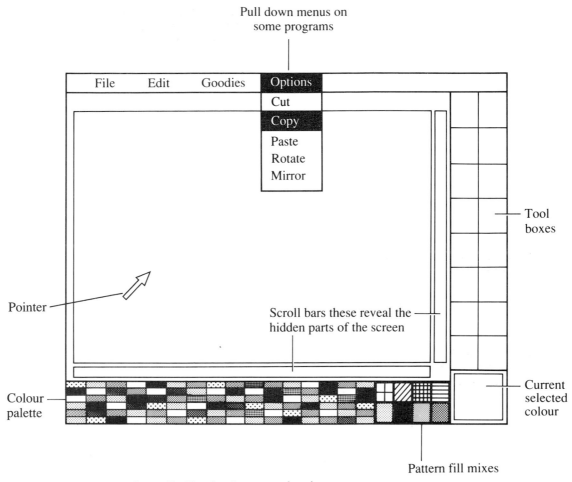

Figure 7   The drawing area and tools

will also be a floating pointer which becomes active when the mouse is moved. At first the layout may appear to be rather confusing almost like going into a strange room. It may help to imagine that you have left your desk to go to the design studio where the tools are organised neatly in boxes around the edge of the room. The pointer is the key to the various tool boxes in the design studio.

Depending on the program you are using the screen may look slightly different but many of the features will be the same. The following list outlines the key tools most commonly on offer in an art program.

Key tools

- Airbrush – this is normally represented by an aerosol can or a group of dots and is used for spraying areas of the screen. (See figure C1 on page 97 in the colour section for an illustration of an airbrush effect.)

- Colour palette – this is not a tool but a 'menu' or list of options. The colour palette which is available on most modern computers is quite extensive.

The palette may be on view all the time or can be called-up by clicking the menu button on the mouse (see figure 8 on page 31). In both cases the colour is selected by directing the pointer at the chosen colour and clicking the mouse button. (See figure C2 on page 97 in the colour section for a colour palette.)

- Cut and paste – this function is normally represented by two overlapping squares and enables areas of the screen to be cut out, rotated, mirrored and pasted into a new location on the screen. This can be a very useful tool for creating repeat patterns and collage work. (See figure C3 on page 98 in the colour section for cut and paste function.)

- Disc – the disc icon is selected when you want to save or retrieve an image. There are a number of variations on this process and it is advisable to consult your program manual for the correct process for your particular computer.

- Geometric shapes – these are represented by circle, square, triangle and ellipse shaped icons. When selected different geometric shapes, either solid or in outline, can be drawn. (See figure C4 on page 98 in the colour section for geometric shapes.)

- Line drawing tools – this function is normally represented by a pencil icon which, when selected, enables you to draw on the screen. The thickness of the pencil line can be changed on some pieces of software. The tone of the pencil is changed by selecting various grey shades from the menu. (See figure C5 on page 98 in the colour section for line drawing tools.)

- Painting tools – painting tools or brushes are normally represented by various different shapes: a circle, square, triangle or ellipse. That is: two curved and two hard-edged brushes. The size of the brush can easily be changed to facilitate fine or bold work. Often the paint tools can also be used as drawing tools. (See figure C6 on page 98 in the colour section for painting tools.)

- Pull down menus – some programs have option menus which are permanently visible at the top of the screen. When one of these is selected by pointing the mouse the menu appears. If you keep your finger pressed on the mouse and move the pointer down the list, each word will be highlighted. Stop at the one you want and click the mouse again to select that feature. (This process is specific to the type of machine you are using.)

- Fill – this function is normally represented by a roller. Colours can be selected from the colour palette and by pointing the roller at an area of the screen and clicking the mouse, areas can be filled with that colour. In addition to this most programs have a pattern fill. The patterns sometimes appear as part of the colour palette and are selected in the same way as above or new patterns can be created to suit a particular idea or design. The patterns can also be used as brushes. (See figure C7 on page 99 in the colour section for fill.)

- Text – the text function is usually represented by the letter A. Once selected text can be typed on the screen by using the keyboard. The text can then be manipulated using the other facilities within the program. With art programs the generation of text is often the weakest feature. On most programs different typefaces or fonts (sets of letters and numbers all of the same typeface and size) are available. (See figure C8 on page 99 in the colour section for text.)

- Watercolour or wash – this function is usually represented by a tap or droplet of water and is not a common feature on most programs. Areas of the screen can be washed over using a transparent brush to create a blurred effect on screen. (See figure C9 on page 99 in the colour section for watercolour or wash.)

- Zoom – this enables a selected area of the screen to be enlarged. Its main function is to facilitate fine detailed work. Details can be refined by changing or adding colour to selected areas pixel by pixel. A pixel is the kind of dot which makes up the image on a computer screen. This can be a long but useful process and the degree to which you would use it would depend on the nature of the work being undertaken. By clicking off zoom you return to your original drawing. Areas of the screen can also be enlarged for creative purposes. (See figure C10 on page 99 in the colour section for zoom.)

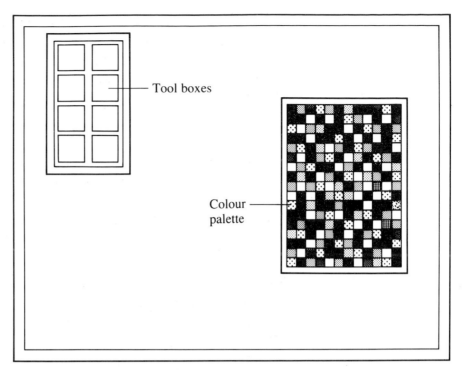

Figure 8 The drawing area with pop-up menus which appear when the menu button is pressed

Criteria for Choosing Software

For work in the art and design areas of the curriculum it is essential to have a computer which operates on the WIMP system (most of the current range of commercial computers now use this system). The following questions may serve as a useful guide when you are choosing software:

- Is the computer the most suitable medium for the activities you wish to undertake?
- Is the program appropriate to the children's needs?
- Is the program open-ended, allowing for full creative activities and development?
- Is the program easy to use?
- Is the screen presentation clear?
- Will all children find it interesting?
- Is the program content free?
- Can different input devices be controlled by the program?

For art and design it is important to choose programs which are open-ended, for instance, programs which provide you with a drawing screen and tools and allow you to decide how best to use them. It is also important to distinguish between Computer Aided Design (CAD) programs and graphic programs. Graphics software is the general name given to all programs used to create images on a computer. CAD programs are designed with a specific purpose in mind and are used to produce technical drawings and architectural illustrations. Desktop publishing programs are used to combine text and images on screen and allow different layouts and designs to be created. Avoid programs which provide you with ready made images of different picture elements as these restrict a child's choice and creativity and a child's control of his/her own artistic vision.

I have now explained what hardware and software are. I will now describe what information technology capability is, so that when you are using an art program you are aware of the IT skills which are being developed.

ART AND INFORMATION TECHNOLOGY CAPABILITY

Information technology can be sub-divided into two distinct areas, firstly, the development of IT is a necessary part of the curriculum in a technological age as computers are now part of our everyday lives at work and in the home. Children need to understand how, why and when it is appropriate to use them. Secondly, IT can be used to enhance the teaching and learning process in most areas of the curriculum.

IT capability should not be confused with computer programming which is the writing of programs, rather it is the application of such programs to particular learning contexts.

It is useful to be aware that IT capability falls into five main strands. The strands assist us in distinguishing different aspects of IT capability and there is a natural overlap in terms of skill development in each strand. The five main strands are:

- communicating ideas;
- handling information;
- modelling;
- measurement and control;
- applications and effects.

Using art programs on the computer leads to computer literacy and children develop skills over a period of time. Most computer work in art and design falls into two of the above areas: communicating ideas and applications and effects.

Communicating ideas

In using an art program children will have opportunities to:

- select items on a computer screen;
- use computer pictures to convey meaning;
- create a drawing on the computer screen and save it to disc;
- use a drawing program to create an image and modify it;
- produce computer images to present information in different forms such as producing a poster, book jacket design, and logo from the same image;
- to use IT to retrieve, develop, organise and present work.

Applications and effects

In using an art program children will have opportunities to discuss and make judgements about the importance of IT in relation to:

- using a computer for tasks which can also be accomplished by other means;
- describing their use of IT and comparing this with other methods of achieving the same result and deciding which was the most effective;
- discussing and reviewing their experience of IT and considering how IT is used in everyday life.

An understanding of the material outlined in this chapter will hopefully give you the contextual framework to comprehend much of the work you and the children do in computer art.

3 The computer and art education

WHAT DOES THE COMPUTER HAVE TO OFFER?

One of the first questions we should ask ourselves is: 'What does the computer have to offer us educationally in the context of art and design education?' As teachers we know that a good art and design education is achieved by fostering and encouraging a lively investigative approach and by giving children opportunities to produce works from observation, memory and their imagination. Through a practical understanding of the elements of art this experience can lead them to an understanding of different art forms, methods and approaches which they can then incorporate into their own work.

Through television, video and computer games, children of all ages are aware of the increasing use of computers. Many of them have daily contact with computers and are familiar with the workings of joysticks, keyboards, mice and printers. Children today have inherited a wider range of environments, possibilities and perceptions than children of previous generations and therefore adapt more readily to the changing world around them. They can often accept change and technical challenge more easily than many adults!

The computer is a wonderfully versatile and effective medium for art. Computers aid drawing and design by allowing images to be easily moved, repeated or enlarged and any mistakes can be easily erased without any loss of face. It can all be part of a pleasurable experience and a first-class teacher of the fact that the process is as important as the end-product! However, the computer alone cannot tell you how to make a creative picture. Children may be able to create different shapes on the screen but they need to acquire other skills in order to manipulate images on the computer and combine and select elements to create a cohesive work of art. They need to know how to fuse the elements of art with computer skills in order to create images ranging from experimental pictures and patterns in the nursery to more sophisticated works for ten- and eleven-year-olds.

A DEVELOPMENTAL APPROACH TO CREATIVE ART AND THE COMPUTER

When working with teachers on computers (both in schools and on inservice courses) I have taken the approach that the creative process sits firmly at the centre of any educational development and the computer merely takes its place alongside other more traditional creative media.

Clearly we all need to make sure that we understand the basic computer skills: how to load a program, save images and use the mouse to move the pointer around the screen in order to select different tools. However, creative work in any medium must not be seen in isolation and this is particularly true of working on a computer when manipulating the tool to create particular effects can, at times, actually get in the way of the creative process and seem like an end in itself. Therefore an appropriate context needs to be defined in order to give meaning to the activity. As the computer alone cannot tell you how to be creative, it is important to develop an approach which has a sound basis in visual education. The three main elements of visual education are perception, use of materials as media and knowledge and understanding. Let us look at each of these elements.

Elements of visual education

- Perception – children should be encouraged to develop their perception by observing and drawing from direct observation, memory and the imagination. They should be encouraged to visualise ideas and draw upon a wide range of resources which they have selected from the natural and made environment.
- Materials as media – children should be able to use the skills and knowledge involved in the process of making and creating. This includes the ability to select and control the use of materials, tools and techniques along with an understanding of the visual language of art and design. They should be encouraged to experiment with colour, line, shape and pattern on a variety of two- and three-dimensional surfaces and be able to develop, express and modify ideas, intentions and feelings.

> • Knowledge and understanding – children should experience delight and pleasure in their own and others' work and have a knowledge of the language of art to help them express their feelings about what they see. They should be encouraged to evaluate their own work and understand how the techniques of other artists and designers can assist them in their development.

These elements are central to any visual education and teacher expertise in these areas is usually well developed. If we ignore such elements when working with computers, the end-products which the children produce may well be dictated by the nature of the programs which they are using.

Experimentation

To participate in a developmental approach we need to experiment, always remembering that this very experimentation and decision making is an important skill in its own right as well as being the process by which we build up the techniques and language of art and design.

When I begin to teach computer art I start by introducing the art program to the whole class. Alternatively, when I have worked alongside other teachers I have worked with smaller groups of children. As you would expect, there are many excited comments as the first brush glides over the screen followed by 'What's the circle for? It would take years to mix that many colours.'

Initially I concentrate on using the drawing and painting tools and changing the brush size and the colour. This is enough for children to take in to begin with and gives everyone ample opportunity to develop some control over the mouse and to become familiar with selecting the tools and colours from the icons on the screen. The children then work in pairs at the computer supporting each other. The difficulties experienced by the children at this stage are minimal; however, I have discovered that those children who have computer games at home have less difficulty controlling the mouse, whilst others find as they experiment, that as the mouse reaches the edge of the mouse mat, the pointer will go no further. I have observed some of these children holding the mouse in the air and rolling the ball that is found underneath it with their fingers. This is a sensible solution to the problem as the pointer continues to move although it also becomes more difficult to control. Alternatively you can pick up the mouse and move it to the opposite side of the mouse mat and start again.

At this early stage, I want the children to use different brush shapes and several colours to create a free design on the screen. I encourage individuals who are tentative to try different brush shapes and assist where necessary if they accidentally click on to one of the other features. There are always individuals who go beyond the initial brief and some competently move into other areas as much by accident as by design. In these initial stages I feel that it is important to keep to specific features but compliment initiative where appropriate and often admire the finished result. The whole approach is experimental and the children take to it readily.

When working with traditional materials rather than the computer I always encourage children to explore their tools and their potential for mark-making before trying to produce representational images. We continue with this process on the computers by making a conscious decision to discourage any kind of conventional image-making in the initial stages so that individuals, whatever their stage of development, feel a sense of achievement.

One of the main benefits of using a computer is the ability to save the images produced. With traditional materials the first marks are often lost. With the computer, many stages in the development of an image can be saved and these can be used at a later stage (either on screen or in printout form) as the basis for a discussion on form, colour, design, or any other element of art. With younger children I talk through the process of saving an image and assist each child. On one occasion a child was heard to say 'Can you save it twice Sir so that I can have one for myself?'. Together we continue this experimental approach by working over previously saved images using other tools from the menu until we have used almost all the available tools. The challenges outlined later in this sector provide a useful guide to extending the children's use of computer tools.

THE NATURE OF A COMPUTER IMAGE

As an electronic medium the computer program can only simulate the use of traditional tools and techniques but it does have other features which are unique to itself. Initially let us consider the nature of a computer image both on the screen and in printout form.

The screen image is illuminated and vibrant and is made up of pixels. Like a newspaper picture where the smaller the dot the better the image so too with the computer screen. Depending on the screen resolution the pixel size will vary; if the screen resolution is high the pixels will be smaller which will make the image finer.

Printouts can be obtained in different sizes, the size being controlled by the program in use. Figures C11, C12 and C13 on page 100 in the colour section show the difference between the different sizes. On small printouts the pixels are compressed, giving the picture a slightly blurred finish. As the printout size increases the pixels become more apparent and the blurring disappears. Another point regarding quality is that the colour of the printout does not always match the colours on screen. This is due to the inability of colour printers (which uses cyan, magenta, yellow and black) to mix the colours on screen (which are made-up of red, green and blue light). This can be avoided by printing out on a very high quality printer which can mix the colours accurately but these are unfortunately beyond the financial constraints of most schools. On most printers, for example, dark blues appear purple and dark reds appear brown. After working on an image for some time it can be disappointing when the printout appears, as the colours may vary and the vibrancy can be lost. Through experience you will begin to identify how different shades of colour suit particular images. Experimentation with different papers is recommended. Figures C14 and C15 on page 101 in the colour section show an image printed on opposite sides of the same quality of paper (the degree of variation is caused by the fact that most quality papers are coated or filled on one side, which improves the printing quality). Figures C16, C17, C18, and C19, on pages 102–3 in the colour section demonstrate how different types of paper can be used as part of an experimental process. Even pieces of fabric can be put through the printer.

COMPARING TRADITIONAL GRAPHIC ART TOOLS AND COMPUTER TOOLS

Art tools		Art program tools
Pencils hard/soft	(see figure 10 overleaf)	Lines of different thickness and tone (see figure 10(a) overleaf)
Charcoal	(see figure 11 on page 41)	Line and tone (see figure 11(a) on page 41)
Paint	(see figure 12 on page 41)	Different brush shapes, colour and spray (see figure 12(a) on page 41)
Watercolour	(see figure 13 on page 42)	Flood facility on some software and blend (see figure 13(a) on page 42)
Wax crayon	(see figure 14 on page 43)	Line, tone and colour (see figure 14(a) on page 43)
Chalk and pastels	(see figure 15 on page 44)	Line, tone and colour (see figure 15(a) on page 44)
Image quality		
Strong textural qualities		Texture becomes pattern
Traditional materials are flexible thick/thin paint		Colour difference between screen and printed image
All traditional materials are sensitive to pressure and density of colour can be achieved		Screen image made up of pixels. Curved lines appear stepped on printouts. Not pressure sensitive. Limit to colour density. Oil pastels have similar qualities to chalk pastels and crayon on the computer. Inks are similar to watercolour.

Figure 9   A comparison of art tools and computer tools

In the chart shown above in figure 9 you can see a comparison between art tools and the equivalent tools available on art programs. Each has its own particular quality which in no way undermines those of the other. The figure numbers and page references shown in brackets in the chart refer you to a comparison of the effects produced by computer and traditional tools. A comparative analysis of the images produced with these tools is interesting.

When using paint, pencil, charcoal or any other graphic tool the user has direct tactile contact with the material. The mouse on a computer is insensitive to pressure so that lines tend to be same strength unless the tone is changed. Likewise the speed at which a graphic tool is used affects the marks it makes. To reproduce this affect, rapid movement of the mouse results in a dotted line on screen, rather than a continuous one. This can be seen in figure C20 on page 104 in the colour section. As the computer image is made up of pixels or squares which cannot recreate a curved line, curved and diagonal lines appear to be stepped. This is particularly evident on printouts, as can be seen in figure C21 on page 105 in the colour section. Through experimentation you will be able to explore the capabilities of computer tools and identify their qualities for yourself.

Figure 10(a)

Figure 10

Figures 10 and 10(a)   A comparison of pencil and its computer equivalent

Figure 11(a)

Figure 11

Figures 11 and 11(a) A comparison of charcoal and its computer equivalent

Figure 12(a)

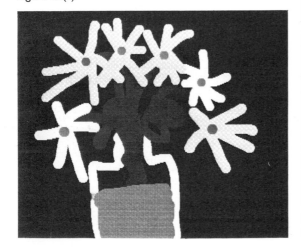

Figures 12 and 12(a) A comparison of paint and its computer equivalent

Figures 13 and 13(a)   A comparison of watercolour and its computer equivalent

Figure 13

Figure 13(a)

Figures 14 and 14(a)   A comparison of wax crayon
and its computer equivalent

Figure 14

Figure 14(a)

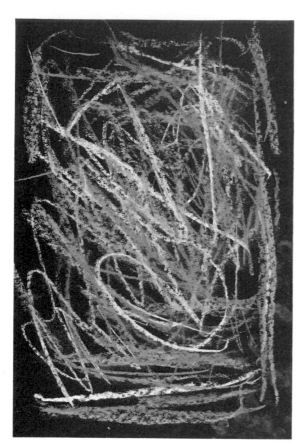

Figures 15 and 15(a) A comparison of chalk pastels and its computer equivalent

Figure 15

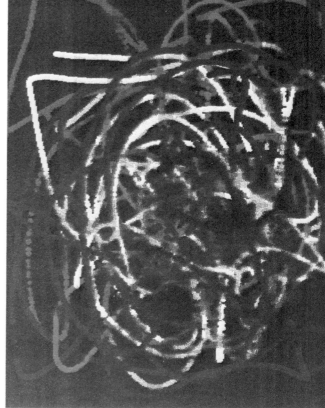

Figure 15(a)

GETTING STARTED

Computer systems vary and you will need to familiarise yourself with how the computer keyboard, monitor, mouse and printer are connected. Figure 16 below is a flow chart giving a general guide to how to 'get started' which is applicable to any computer system and program.

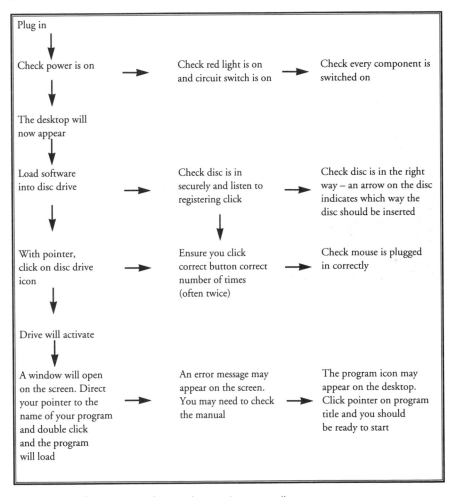

Figure 16   A flow diagram showing how to 'get started'

If problems do arise you may need to seek further help from your computer manual, IT co-ordinator or your computer supplier. Yet many teachers find that it is the children who are able to solve most of the problems which arise!

The chart in figure 17 opposite outlines the basic materials and the main processes which you should be familiar with.

Having familiarised yourself with your equipment, the program and the main tools on offer, there is nothing to stop you and your pupils from experimenting. The following challenges offer a structured guide to some of the most fundamental areas of computer art.

COMPUTER CHALLENGES

It is important for children to become familiar with controlling the mouse before moving on to more structured work. Initial free experimentation should assist this process. (See figure C22 on page 105 in the colour section.) I have outlined a number of challenges which offer a structure for getting started. They are suitable for use with all children but it is vital that each child experiences success at every stage. Therefore, if children are experiencing difficulty they need to be given time to consolidate their work before being moved on to the next challenge. Likewise, if they discover something new, let them explore it before slowly moving them back on to the original task. If the following series of challenges is followed many elements of computer art will be explored.

I would recommend that during the initial free experimentation stage only one of the children's images is saved. When working on the challenges I would suggest that each child saves up to three stages. These can then be used as a basis for a discussion on the processes involved. Afterwards, ask each child to talk about their image either on the screen or in printout form. What did they do? What did they like?

In the following challenges I have tried to use the same language as I would use when working with children. The language we use is, of course, very important as it will help to build up a child's vocabulary for describing the computer image. The children should work through the challenges in pairs supporting each other as they are working. Lastly, it is, of course, very important to have tried out each of the challenges yourself so that you can discuss with the individual child the kind of marks which are being made.

What you need

A computer system

An art program – make a backup copy of your program to work from. Check with your IT co-ordinator or handbook for correct procedure. Store the original safely. You are not allowed to make multiple copies (see copyright on page 81). It is safer to work from a backup of the program. If it gets damaged you can always make another from the original.

Main skills required

Formatting discs – you will need blank formatted discs to store images. Newly purchased discs are not formatted. Formatting is simply the term used to describe the way the computer organises the disc so that it can store information or data. Discs formatted on one make of computer cannot be used on other machines as each computer system formats in a slightly different way. Check with your IT co-ordinator or consult your computer handbook for the correct procedure. It is advisable to have a number of formatted discs available when you start as children's work could be lost if there is nothing to save it on to. When a disc is full the computer will tell you. Have another one ready! Avoid saving images on to the program disc.

Saving images – this process will vary depending on which program you are using. Consult your program handbook for the correct procedure. Save successive images incrementally i.e. picture, picture 1, picture 2 etc. In doing this you will be able to follow the development of an image. Get in to the habit of saving images frequently or valuable work could be lost. Allow and encourage the children to save their own work.

Retrieving previously saved images – as above each program will have its own procedure. Consult your program handbook. Remember you must load your program disc before you try to load previous images.

Deleting previously saved images – consult your program handbook.

Printing – a colour printer is essential. Most programs allow printouts in up to three different sizes. Usually the progam has its own printer driver. This is a program within the main program which controls the printer. There will be a facility for selecting the type of printer you are using along with the size option, small, medium or large (A3). As most colour printers are not very wide an A3 printout will be in two pieces which will need pasting together. Larger printouts can be obtained by using a scaling facility on some programs. Consult your program handbook.

Figure 17   Chart showing the basic materials and processes

Challenge 1(a) – mark-making

- Find the picture of the pencil from the menu.
- Choose a colour and draw.
- Now make your pencil thicker and draw with it. Now make it thinner.
- Find the thinnest line you can make, find the thickest.
- Now choose a different shaped pencil and do the same as before. Compare these marks with the previous marks.
- Repeat what you have just done with other shapes.
- Draw a curved line slowly and carefully. Now draw another curve quickly. Compare them.
- Note: You should notice that the line drawn quickly across the computer screen appears fragmented. This is due to the inability of the mouse and screen to cope with rapid movement.

Challenge 1(b) – coloured marks

- A similar challenge might be to focus on colour. Let the children choose a primary colour and find as many different shades of that colour as they can. Get them to create marks with it. Discuss the different shades with the children. This could extend into vocabulary work on colour. Let them explore the multicoloured or dithered pencil if it is available. Restrict the number of colours which make-up the pencil and compare different effects. Explore hot/cold colours, moods and seasons. Figure C36 on page 118 shows how a colour is affected when its surrounding colour changes.
- Note: It is also interesting to note that when coloured lines overlap the one underneath is wiped out. (See figure C20 on page 104 in the colour section.)

Challenge 2 – geometric shapes

- Choose a geometric shape.
- Now fill the screen with a variety of different sized shapes.
- Now add other shapes so that some overlap.
- Find the fill option on the menu (the roller) and fill some of the shapes and some of the spaces. Observe the effects.
- Fill some of the shapes using a pattern fill or create your own patterns in the shapes or spaces.
  (See figure C23 on page 106 in the colour section.)

Challenge 3 – painting

- Choose a season and think about the colours and shapes that you would use to describe it.
- Use the experiences gained in challenges 1 and 2 to create an abstract interpretation of that season.
- Divide the screen into four sections and use different brushes, sizes and shapes to create an impression of each season.
- Note: Similar themes might revolve around the elements, moods or festivals. By using the right kind of descriptive language the computer can become a vehicle for expressive work.
  (See figure C24 on page 107 in the colour section.)

Challenge 4 – watercolour or wash

- Work with one colour and cover part of the screen with shades of it.
- Use the watercolour brush and go round the edges of the shapes you have made. The edges will appear softer and there will be a slight colour change.
  (See figure C25 on page 108 of the colour section.)

Challenge 5 – airbrush

- Find the spray facility and explore the effect of different densities.
- Introduce another colour and experiment with it.
- Look at a postcard or a slide of an impressionist picture. Select a section to interpret.
- Look at your section and see which colour has been used the most. Now choose this colour and fill the screen with it.
- Use the spray to make your own impressionistic effect.
- You do not have to copy the picture exactly but use the picture as a starting point for your own ideas.
- Note: it might be interesting if the same postcard were used by the whole class and each child's printout used to create a large impressionistic collage.
  (See figure C26 on page 108 in the colour section.)

Challenge 6 – cut and paste or copy

- Choose one of your previous images.
- Select the cut and paste tool from the menu.
- Decide on the area of the image that you want to copy.
- Place the pointer at the top left-hand corner of the area to be copied.
- Press and hold down the mouse button and drag a box over the chosen area.
- When the mouse is released a clear floating shape will be evident. This shape moves as the mouse is moved.
- Position the shape on the chosen part of the screen and press the mouse button again.
- The cut section will appear.
- Experiment with this facility to create an interesting design.
  (See figure C27 on page 109 in the colour section.)

Challenge 7 – zoom or enlarge

- Find the zoom facility and zoom into an area of the picture.
- The screen image will change showing large pixels. You could experiment by changing the colour of each pixel or by using the spray before going back to the normal screen to observe the effects.
- This is described as editing part of the picture.
- Cut out a small section of the screen and scale it. The effect will be similar to the zoom (edit) only this time the picture will remain.
  (See figures C28 and C28(a) on page 110 in the colour section.)

Challenge 8 – text

- Select the text icon from the menu.
- Create a design using the initials of your name.
- Position the pointer at the point where you want your letters to be. Use the keyboard to type letters on the screen.
- Use the other features which you have explored to create an interesting design, for instance: cut and paste, enlarge, mirror etc.
  (See figure C8 on page 99 in the colour section.)

4 Image-making – traditional methods and the computer

INTRODUCTION

Any creative activity in any medium involves using our emotions to express the way we feel about the world around us. In our everyday lives we respond to, and express our ideas of, visual and other sensual experiences. These help us to build up a picture of ourselves in relation to each other and the environment in which we live.

As teachers it is important for us to have an understanding of the processes which help us to develop artistic learning. The question we need to ask ourselves is, 'How do we use the computer alongside the traditional media with which we are all familiar and how does it fit in to a developmental art programme?'

I hope to supply some answers to this question in the course of this chapter by assessing the different art processes which are appropriate to a computing medium and by comparing the limitations and advantages of this new medium in relation to the traditional art forms.

THE DEVELOPMENT OF CHILDREN'S IMAGERY

Our expectations of children's imagery should not differ from the norm just because a computer is being used rather than a graphic tool. It is therefore important that we know something of the normal developmental stages in a child's use of imagery.

As children develop their imagery falls into three main categories irrespective of the tool being used. These are outlined below.

- Scribble (two–five-years-old) – experimenting with tools and materials.
- Symbolic (four–seven-years-old) – making drawings using different tools.
- Analytic (seven–years-old and above) – striving for visual realism.

(Experimenting with tools and materials applies to all of the stages above, regardless of the child's age and ability.)

Scribble, the first of these, occurs when young children first learn to grasp a graphic tool. Initially, they make marks with it in an accidental way as it moves across the paper. At a later stage this will develop into a more conscious realisation of the types of marks which are made. During the symbolic stage children select from what they know based on sensory experience. Some children quite naturally continue in this mode and use it in many ways and alongside their later analytical developments, other children show potential for visual analysis from an early age. Before children begin to read, their images provide a language to describe the world in which they live through the shapes and symbols which they create. This is true whatever the media.

Older children in the analytical stage seem to strive for visual realism becoming more critical of their work and that of others, through an increasing need to match and compare in both two- and three-dimensions. It would appear that they begin to analyse, becoming increasingly concerned with the interpretation of line, form, pattern and texture. It is at this stage that the teacher must plan for challenges and investigations through the senses of looking and touching as well as encouraging children to use language to explore and discuss their work.

Children are individuals, so there are obviously exceptions to every rule. It is important to bear in mind that the age at which they pass through some or all of these stages will vary according to their emotional and physical maturity and the breadth of their experience. Some children may stay at a particular stage or be several years behind their peers in their development. The sensitive teacher will monitor the child's progress and response to different tools and materials and will find out the most appropriate way to assist that child's development. This applies to the use of computers as it does to the use of any other tools.

At whatever stage a child may be, it is always important to remember how central a part art plays in children's lives. I have seen children experience delight when they use an art program for the first time. Lines, shapes and colours can be placed quickly on the screen allowing numerous patterns to be created in a short space of time. There is also an element of magic as one cannot see the tool that one is using but it is there, activated by pressing the mouse button. It is upon this delight that we must capitalise, allowing children to experiment and experience a wide range of creative processes.

CHOOSING THE RIGHT MEDIUM

Children have a natural inclination to do representational drawings when they use an art program and although the immediacy of the results and the colour may initially excite them they can become frustrated by the resultant image. However, the child who already possesses a rich experience of art and an understanding of the facilities of an art program, can find drawing on the computer, for instance, a challenging and rewarding experience. A seven-year-old's comment was:

> I like going on the computer but it is easier to use a pencil. The reason I like going on the computer is you can get water colours where on some paper you can't.

This child has already started to weigh up the suitability of one medium against another.

Sometimes the computer can be used as a starting point for art or project work which then develops using more traditional media. For example, the project on seasons illustrated in figures C29 and C29(a) on page 111 in the colour section show how winter colours have been selected and used to create a pattern picture. At other times the computer can serve to explore another subject area as part of a process. Figures C30 and C30(a) on page 112 of the colour section illustrate such a process. A drawing of a shell preceded the work shown (a computer image) which was then developed into a print on fabric. This process therefore involved drawing with a graphic tool, the computer and textiles. A computer image can also be used as an end in itself. The picture 'Landscape after Monet' in figure C26 on page 108 in the colour section was such a project. Thus the computer can be used at the beginning of a project, as part of a process and as an end in itself, it can stand alone or be integrated into a wider exploration of a number of artistic media. It is as versatile as we choose to make it. An eleven-year-old made these comments about her use of the computer and in so doing explains very clearly the versatility which makes computer art so attractive to many children:

I have used the computer to do drawings from the age of four and I enjoy using other materials but find the computer an interesting way to work. Sometimes it is hard to control the mouse and do detailed pictures. I like all of the different thicknesses of the brushes and I like using the zoom to look closely at the picture. I also like it when you can cut out a part of your picture and put it in lots of different places which you couldn't do normally. I like the effects you get that look like ink or charcoal and when you blur your picture. I had seen some toys arranged at an antique fair and I thought it would be interesting to do a picture using my own teddy bear. I set up a still life with my teddy bear in it and then drew it out roughly on the computer, then I added a bit more detail and then began to colour the picture in. I coloured in my teddy bear first and used the spray to get the darker patches on, then I coloured in the picture and picture frame and finally did the flowers and jar. I added shadowing and more detail when it was needed and coloured the cloth in, then I gave the picture in the picture frame a glassy look by adding lines of light colours over it for a reflection.

Figures C31–C31(c) on page 113 in the colour section show how this girl built-up a sequence of images by saving each image before refining the next. She printed out each stage and was able to discuss the processes involved.

The following section tries to show how the computer can be used alongside traditional media, as in practice areas of experience will overlap naturally.

DRAWING: TRADITIONAL MEDIA OR COMPUTER?

Drawing is a means of communicating using marks with tools which can include pencil, crayon, charcoal, chalk, pen-brushes, fingers and the computer. It is also a means of communicating which we use at all stages of our development.

Initially, in their early years, children will make random marks whilst exploring their media, but eventually they will discover images by accident and will invent subject matter. When using art programs they enjoy watching the coloured lines appear clearly and instantly. At this stage in their development it is important to let the child have many attempts during one session whether it is using the pen, pencil or an art program. Just as you may vary the paper you offer the children to work on you can offer a choice of coloured backgrounds on the screen.

Figure 18   First mark-making, exploring line, by a six-year-old boy

At a later stage in their development, a child will create drawings which describe how they think of themselves and how they perceive the world around them, these can be called 'story pictures'. They use circles and oval shapes and could select these shapes from the computer, or create their own. Children may use different sizes of brush and pencil and can change their colours readily. They may wish to change part of an image. An eraser may be available on the computer if that is the tool they are using but there are various other strategies as well. The UNDO facility on most programs can be used to erase the last coloured mark made. Alternatively they can work over the image with another colour similar to applying new paint over dry paint. Another strategy is to match the same background colour from the palette.

Figure 19 'Outside my house' a story picture, by a six-year-old girl

As children become more interested in fine detail they will produce story pictures and scenes which are more realistic than those produced at an earlier stage of development. Firsthand experience is essential and they become more interested in analysing what they are drawing. They will want to match colours accurately and develop more of an awareness of the elements of line, form, tone, shape, texture and pattern. Proportion and depth are qualities which the children try to achieve in their pictures.

In my experience with computers I have found that some children who have well developed drawing skills can become despondent because it is more difficult to achieve accuracy with a mouse that it is with a pencil, as the former is harder to control. One way round this is to use the method outlined below and opposite which was used to create the portrait in figures 20 and 20(a, b and c) which was translated on to the computer from a drawing. An acetate sheet was placed over the drawing and traced using an overhead projector pen. The acetate sheet was then sellotaped to the computer screen and used as the pattern. We found that this was the quickest way of getting the image on to the screen. This method can be used to translate many different images and is similar to the way we use tracing paper. This allows children in the analytical stage to benefit from the advantages of the computer whilst retaining the visual realism which they can achieve with graphic tools.

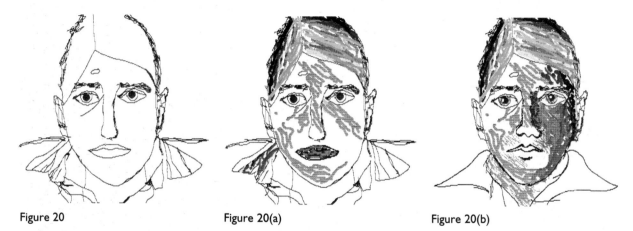

Figure 20   Figure 20(a)   Figure 20(b)

Figures 20 and 20(a,b)   A sequence of three pictures showing how a portrait was built-up on screen after using an acetate to translate a drawing on to the screen, by a ten-year-old boy

Children must proceed at their own pace and the quest to look and question must be theirs not ours although teachers are obviously the catalysts who direct their attention towards particular elements. Pattern is a good starting point for children at all stages as they can look for circles, squares, straight lines, repeats, symmetry, similarities and differences.

Children need a variety of objects (both natural and made) to observe and handle and access to reference materials such as photographs, postcards and prints. Figures C32, C33, C33(a), and C34(a)–(d) on pages 114–17 in the colour section, are all exciting examples of children exploring drawing using both traditional and computer mediums.

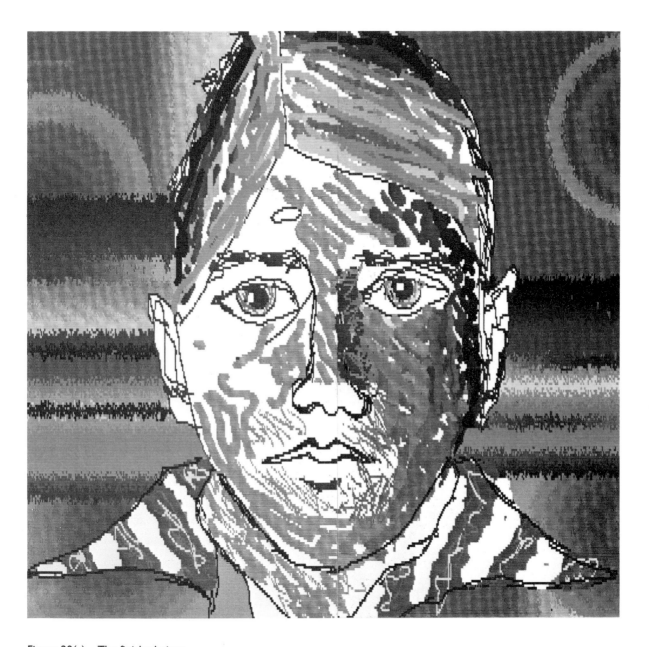

Figure 20(c)   The finished piece

A drawing project: exploring line with a reception class

This project was undertaken with reception children with the aim of giving them an opportunity to experiment with line in a variety of media. The computer was introduced not as an unusual media but merely as one of many.

I worked with the classteacher and encouraged the children to draw freely using pencil and charcoal. To support this we looked at drawings by Van Gogh and Seurat and discussed the kinds of marks which they had made. The next step was to continue this experimental approach by working on the computer.

The children were given a brief introduction to the art program, we explained how the computer drawing area was laid out, which screen icons represented the drawing tools and how to change the colours by pointing the cursor and clicking the mouse button. We deliberately instructed the children to work with the drawing tools and encouraged them to express themselves in the same way as they had done with the traditional tools.

The children's excitement was evident as their tentative first movements were replaced by sweeping gestures. It wasn't long before they wanted to extend their scribble drawings by filling in areas with the fill tool.

Teacher observations
The first child worked quickly and intensely and didn't speak apart from saying that the work reminded him of a string pattern.

The second child expressed herself with the following lengthy dialogue as she worked.

I've chosen red, now I've put it back on green and now blue again. Now I'll choose brown ... it looks like a flower. Now you can't see yellow properly. Can we change this a different colour? [I showed her the roller (fill tool), she then proceeded to fill in certain areas.] Now I want another green, a light green. Now I want a dark colour. [She selected purple, then deep blue.] It doesn't look like the picture I started with, that little bit there [she pointed to the screen] reminds me of a pink umbrella. I want to choose some more colours so I'll fill in all the white spaces. I like using the computer, its nice to draw with, its easier to colour.

The third child worked quickly and quietly, she used the mouse skilfully maintaining control and selecting specific colours. When she had completed her work she said: 'I like the bright colours.'

The fourth child had poor motor skills and a short concentration span and was generally difficult to motivate. Initially he had difficulty controlling the mouse, he kept going outside the frame. When he moved the cursor back on to the screen he started doing short, jagged, sharp movements. I asked what he was doing to which he replied 'colouring in'. I showed him how to use the roller and he was delighted with the quick outcome. He made excited noises each time he filled in an area with colour. 'It's much easier to colour in than with pencils.'

The fifth child initially had difficulty controlling the cursor, she kept building on top of previous patterns. She then realised that she could make circular movements and really enjoyed the feel of the motion.

The follow-up

When the exercise had been completed the children used their drawings and computer printouts as a starting point for some simple relief printmaking. We had previously introduced the children to monoprinting, now each child was given a small piece of card and some string. They translated the lines into a relief pattern by sticking the string on to the card. The cards would later be used as the printing blocks. The whole class then looked at a range of prints by artists such as Hokusai, Klee and Warhol. We looked at different print qualities and explained that with printing it was possible, unlike a painting, to create more than one image. We found that Warhol's repeat images of the 'Soup Can' and 'Marilyn Monroe' were useful in

Figure 21

Figure 21(a)

Figure 21(b)

Figures 21 and 21(a,b)   Developing line drawings on the computer into relief print blocks, making prints and then collaging them together to make a whole-class frieze, by five-year-old children

explaining this and the children were excited by the prospect of producing a repeated print just like an established artist. We also pointed out that the computer printouts were also a form of printing.

After finishing the printing we decided to press the blocks into clay and again emphasised the possibility of making several clay tiles from each block. Finally the blocks were assembled together, complete with ink and clay deposit and this was displayed with the prints, drawings, computer printouts and clay tiles. Together they demonstrated the full range of processes that we had been through.

Advantages of the computer

- Fast and easy access to a variety of tools.
- Zoom facility allows details to be added to an image.
- Patterns can be developed from drawings by using the cut and repeat facility.
- Computers can be used like a pencil to draw directly from observation.
- Different stages can be saved to disc.

Limitations of the computer

- The mouse is harder to control than the pencil.
- The excitement created by the colour and the facilities available can be distracting.
- It is important for children to have explored the computer first before you ask them for a line drawing.
- There are no facilities which replace the unique quality which other drawing materials offer.

COLOUR: TRADITIONAL MEDIA OR COMPUTER?

Colour is a powerful expressive element and has an important part to play in all areas of artistic experience and includes the use of paint, dyes, inks, pastel crayons, fabrics, threads and the computer. It is probably the element we respond to most strongly. Colour is capable of activating feelings in all of us and we use it to reflect our feelings and moods and to decorate our environment and ourselves.

Children's paintings are frequently full of expressive qualities. They will paint as they feel whereas when they draw they are more inclined to draw what they know or see. Paint has a particularly expressive quality which is not matched by any other medium to which children usually respond. Children often become excited when mixing colour and creating new colours and they respond to the immediacy of moving wet and thick paint across a surface.

The computer tools – pencils, brushes, spray, watercolour, fill and the extensive colour palette – offer many opportunities for exploring colour and its effects as figure C35 illustrates. ('After Van Gogh' on page 118 in the colour section.) It can be interesting to look at the work of recognised artists in order to discuss how they have used paint and how they have achieved particular effects.

Some useful comparisons can be made by trying to interpret images by the juxtaposition of the colours they use. Children can see how colours play with each other by selecting different coloured backgrounds and comparing them. Figure C36 on page 118 in the colour section illustrates this. If you half close your eyes and look at each colour in turn you will see a difference in the size and intensity of the image. This exercise can be easily set up by the teacher using the repeat facility and can be used with children of all ages. The outlines of the blue shapes become sharper against the light, bright colours. The shapes appear blurred against a dark background. The colour influences the appearance of the shape and the strength of the background.

Colours can give you different sensations and stimulate a range of impressions such as evoking sounds and emotions. They can remind you of smell, taste and atmosphere. On the computer screen you can run through colours easily and the children may describe them as hot, cold, friendly, sharp and by numerous other names. Colour is integral to all aspects of art and you will find many more examples of how colour has been used in the colour section. Figure C37 on page 119 in the colour section shows how colour has been used to create a particular mood.

Advantages of the computer

- A wide choice of colours are on offer and they can be selected quickly.
- Adjustments can be made to an image as required.
- The process itself can involve changing ideas, whilst the development of the work can be shown, including the decision making, by saving the work on to disc and printing out.

- Through discussing their images the children can develop their vocabulary in regard to colour.
- The luminosity of the computer screen gives the image a dramatic strength of colour, specially when used against a dark background.

Limitations of the computer

- Colour mixing on screen is only available on some programs.
- Real paintings have tactile qualities and can offer a textural dimension which adds to their expressive quality.
- With traditional materials a variety of paint and paint surfaces can be used whilst on a computer texture can only be represented as pattern.

PRINTMAKING: TRADITIONAL MEDIA OR COMPUTER?

Printmaking naturally develops from looking at different textured surfaces with children. In essence printmaking is about creating more than one image. As we have seen with other aspects of artistic learning there is a sequence to the development of printmaking. Any scrap or junk material such as cotton reels, foil or leaves can be used for initial experiments. These first attempts are important. Dipping these objects in paint and then stamping the shapes out is an exciting experience. We can then move on to more precise work such as monoprinting, potato printing and computer printing. A computer image can be printed out many times which makes it an excellent tool for printing, comparable to printing from a traditional lino or wood block. The same image can be reduced in size and repeated in multiple forms on screen. Alternatively a repeat/tile facility on some programs allows any area of the screen to be cut out and repeated to create a tile pattern. The image can then be manipulated further using the mirror facility to make a pattern repeat. (See figure C38 on page 119 in the colour section.) It is important that the work should reflect the age of the child. Start with simple geometric designs which can be translated into press prints.

Advantages of the computer

- Any screen image can be reduced in scale and turned into a repeat pattern.
- Many colour combinations can be explored in a short space of time.
- Different stages in the production of a design can be saved and printed.
- Printouts offer opportunities for discussion about choices of different design stages that can be revisited if appropriate.

Limitations of the computer

- Complex patterns may be difficult to translate into other art media.
- There are limitations on the size of the printout – designs may have to be enlarged on a photocopier to be used for further work.
- Too many choices can be confusing; challenges should be focused on particular themes.

COLLAGE AND TEXTURE: TRADITIONAL MEDIA OR COMPUTER?

Collages can be made out of almost any materials including threads and fibres, paper, card, string, wood, twigs, fur, feathers, seeds, seed heads, dried grasses and plants, buttons, sequins, leather, and fabrics. Children can become very excited when handling different materials as they abound in colour, pattern and texture and can be a way of making a pattern or story picture into a three-dimensional picture.

In the early stages of working with collage the activities are primarily those of sorting according to various attributes. (See figure C39 and C39(a) on page 120 in the colour section.) Using this activity the potential for developing visual discrimination is endless. Children may sort according to different types if patterns or textures are predominant or they may sort according to colour, tone or feel.

67

During the sorting there are opportunities for the children to talk about and discuss the different qualities of the materials. Children should be encouraged to bring in their own found objects as these objects will be familiar to them and the materials they collect for themselves will often have strong visual attractions and can be used as a starting point for computer work.

Any picture created using an art program can be manipulated in different ways to create a pattern or collage effect. Sections can be enlarged or reduced, colours can be changed, and parts of one picture can be cut and pasted on to another.

In order to facilitate further progression a printout of the complete image can be cut into sections and collaged in conjunction with more traditional materials.

Texture on a computer becomes pattern. Figures C40, and C40(a, b, and c) on page 121 in the colour section illustrate a computer

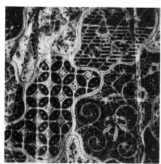

Figure 22

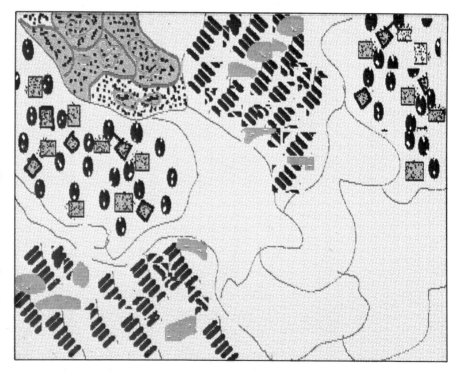

Figure 22(a)

Figures 22 and 22(a)   Batik pattern based on an Indian fabric design, by a ten-year-old boy and girl

project on shape and pattern which can be undertaken with different age groups. The children were asked to select a shape and fill it with as many colours and patterns as they could find. They were then printed out, cut and collaged on to hardboard. The children were then asked to match the textures using paint over the top of their collage.

Advantages of the computer

- All art programs offer opportunities for cut and paste. Sections can be cut out and enlarged, relocated or rotated.
- Colours can be matched or juxtaposed at speed. Sections of designs can be cut out and used to fill other areas.
- Any area of the screen can be cut out and pasted.
- Different stages can be saved to disc.

Limitations of the computer

- High speed image processing can lead to too many choices and therefore challenges should be focused on particular themes: hot or cold colours, or pattern repeats.

TEXTILES: TRADITIONAL MEDIA OR COMPUTER?

As with collage, you should let the children explore their materials in order to examine their properties and potential. Let them pull the threads and fibres and see if they can undo them or twist them. When exploring textiles the children may begin to question how they were made. Such a discussion can lead to activities such as sticking, wrapping, knotting, sewing, dyeing and weaving. Encourage the children to bring in garments or fabrics from home as they can be used for display purposes and can be particularly exciting if a diversity of cultures are represented and used as they are in figures 22 and 22(a) opposite.

A water project with textiles and computers

This project was carried out by a class of seven-year-olds. Their topic theme for the term was water and before starting to work on the computer they had looked at many images and discussed the way that water flows, the colours, reflections, ripples and light. They had also done some experiments with paint to convey the feeling of flowing movement.

Despite their limited experience on the computer the children found little difficulty in working with the mouse and after a short while developed confidence in selecting items from the screen. We began by looking at the basic tools and each child experimented for a short while before we began to look at the theme. We looked again at images of water by artists like Hockney, Monet and Hokusai and at photographs showing different reflections.

For the initial experimentation the children worked in pairs and supported each other. We continued in this way with each child in turn, encouraging them to convey their feelings about water by using the tools and colours available. Teacher intervention was minimal, being limited to suggestions to try a different colour or try the blend brush to blur edges. Occasionally an individual had to be reminded which mouse button to press but these occasions were rare. There was a feeling of excitement amongst the children as the images were produced. It was clear that they were learning from each other by discussing ways to create particular effects. The resulting images were then translated into print collage or weaving using a range of materials which the children were familiar with. (See figures C41–C41(e) on pages 122–3 in the colour section.) In such a project, traditional media and computer are used in conjunction to produce work of a very high standard and educational value.

Advantages of the computer

- Screen images can be reduced in scale and turned into repeat patterns.
- Many colour combinations can be explored in a short space of time.

- Different stages in the production of a design can be saved and printed.
- Printouts offer opportunities for discussion about choices of different design stages that can be revisited if appropriate.
- Work should reflect the age of the child. Start with simple geometric designs which can be translated into press prints.

Limitations of the computer

- Complex patterns may be difficult to translate into other art media.
- There are limitations on the size of the printout — designs may have to be enlarged on a photocopier to be used for further work. Most photocopiers are still black and white so in scaling up one loses the colour input.

WORK IN THREE-DIMENSIONS: TRADITIONAL MEDIA OR COMPUTER?

Three-dimensional or 3D work in most primary schools is a skill given less status than it deserves. Young children may often be involved in 'junk modelling' but the focus is usually on representing an object rather than using the materials to create abstract structures which can lead to an understanding of the materials used. Our foundation for knowledge and understanding of 3D is left to our experience of living in a 3D world because most art activities are still two-dimensional (2D). There is a belief that 2D work often precedes 3D work and whilst some artists may work in this way, most don't. It is essential that children, especially young children, explore the nature of the materials that they are given and discover what the materials can do by working with them in both two- and three-dimensions.

Collage techniques and 3D work have much in common. One aim in collage is to sort out one pattern, area, material or colour from another in a purposeful rather than an accidental way. The purpose is to produce a piece of work which has unity and this also applies to 3D work. The children consider contrast, unity, balance and so on through experimentation and discussion. This could also be illustrated by looking at the work of sculptors or at many twentieth century canvases which have 3D qualities. This is because many twentieth century canvases are heavily loaded with paint or have objects stuck into the paint making them into relief sculptures. Often, the difference between painting, relief and sculpture cannot be defined easily.

Stitching 3D forms to a painting or a piece of computer work is one way in which mixed media work can first arise and there is much to be gained from translating an idea from one dimension to another.

Once a 3D model has been constructed it can be viewed from a multiplicity of viewpoints. This requires the viewer or object to move, but an alternative is to produce a design on the computer showing various interesting angles, or a collage could be made of several computer images showing different angles.

Many children play computer games at home and some of these games have 3D effects. When using an art program children find that some of the basic facilities also produce a 3D effect, for instance the paintbrush loaded with different coloured paint and the moving shapes. Once the children had discovered these facilities they were very keen to use and exploit them. A certain depth was evident in their pictures and patterns which clearly pleased them. (See figures C42 and C42(a) on page 124 in the colour section.)

Leigh pressed a button and the whole screen went black and white. Leigh pressed another button and the spiral came up.

Some computer programs can produce more sophisticated 3D effects by rotating shapes and viewing objects from different angles, but the value of this is more relevant to older children engaged in design projects. It is an area which could be explored but it requires some expertise and if one remembers how little time a child will spend on an art activity on the computer I feel that the time could be better spent on other activities.

Advantages of the computer

- A computer's processing power allows complex shapes to be rotated and viewed on the screen.
- By using the right programs children can gain an awareness of depth, shape and space.

Limitations of the computer

- Difficult area to develop using a basic art program.
- Requires the use of dedicated software.

DESIGN: TRADITIONAL MEDIA OR COMPUTER?

There are a number of qualities which are required by those involved in designing and each is of equal importance; they include those listed below.

- An awareness of spatial relationships – how objects, images and systems fit together in terms of size and shape and how they might be rearranged or manipulated to create different results.
- Visual awareness – an ability to observe particular arrangements of objects and to be able to criticise and appreciate their shape and form.
- An awareness of materials – to have an understanding of various materials and to understand their differences. To be able to choose appropriate materials and processes.

Design work can be two- or three-dimensional and therefore can be developed throughout the primary curriculum. Design is a part of all art activities. The following project is a good example of how graphic design work can be experienced with both traditional media and computers.

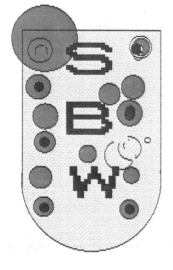

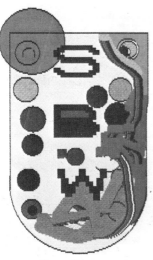

Logo project

The logos reproduced below and in the colour section were produced by nine- and ten-year-old children as part of a project on signs and symbols. After looking at commercially designed logos which the children had provided, we discussed how we could design a logo using our own initials. We decided that the logo had to be personal and should include one or more of our favourite pastimes. We began by designing on paper and then the children worked in pairs on the computer. First they explored the potential of the different tools and then, still in pairs, supported each other in translating their drawing on to the computer screen. They used the drawing tools to get the basic image on to the screen and then the cut, paste and scale facilities to move, enlarge or reduce parts of the image to create the desired effect. In some cases we used part of the screen as a sketch-pad and cut and pasted sections into the logo shape. All stages of the design process were printed out to demonstrate the different processes. Often the final logo design was further reduced to see what effect it had on the image. On one occasion we traced letters on to an acetate sheet, taped it to the computer screen and traced round it using the mouse. Once completed the logos were translated on to a fabric panel using collage materials. The individual panels were assembled to create a large wall hanging. Figures 23 and 23(a) show two of the logos. A sequence showing the different stages in one boy's design process can be seen in figures C43–C43(c) and the wall hanging composed of all of the logos is shown in figure C44. These figures are on pages 125–6 in the colour section.

When the wall hanging was displayed alongside the computer images it was interesting to listen to the children discussing the differences and similarities between the two. This shows how the children's ideas had developed and how they required different ways of designing when working with different materials and media. On both occasions the children had worked creatively with the tools provided focusing on the design element (line, shape and layout) and yet exploring the textural qualities when working with textiles.

Figure 23

Figures 23 and 23(a)   Different logos from the logo project, by nine- and ten-year-old children

Figure 23(a)

Advantages of the computer

- Different ideas can be tried out quickly before deciding on a particular design.
- Cut and paste facilities can be used to isolate a particular area of the picture.
- The scaling facility can be used to increase or decrease the size of the design allowing it to be used for different purposes.
- Different stages in the development of the design can be saved.
- Many different colour combinations can be tried.
- Selected images can be printed and can then form the basis of discussion for further development.

> ## Limitations of the computer
> - Too many choices can be offered causing confusion.
> - There are limitations on the size of the printout for certain types of work; designs may have to be enlarged on a photocopier to be used for further work.

RESPONDING TO ARTEFACTS: TRADITIONAL MATERIALS OR COMPUTER?

All children are artists when they create their own images in order to express their feelings about the world around them. But children also find great excitement in looking at the work of other artists and are fascinated by how they compose works and use different materials to express their ideas. You can talk to the children about the kinds of marks and gestures the artist has made whether it be in paint, clay, wood or any other media. This approach helps them to develop a language which enables them to describe the elements of art.

The computer is an ideal medium for interpreting the work of others, for example, if you were focusing on colour you could look at Matisse cut outs to see the different effects the colours have (see figure C36 on page 118 in the colour section). Ask the children to interpret a painting on the computer by using a limited range of tools. They have done this in figure C45 on page 126 in the colour section which shows how the spray facility has been used to create an impressionistic effect. Another challenge might be to focus on colour, for instance: match the colours on screen to a painting or, alternatively, focus on pattern. Figures C46–C46(e) on page 127 in the colour section show how a seven-year-old child has interpreted Henri Rousseau's *Tropical storm with a tiger (Surpris!)*. It is interesting how the brush shapes have been used to describe the leaves and how carefully the colours have been matched. It is clear that she has used all her skill and experience, developed through free exploration and challenges, to produce this striking image. Work in this area can be extended by using digitised images of artefacts or paintings. A digitiser is an input device which enables pictures to be loaded into different programs to be manipulated. Digitised images of paintings offer opportunities for discussion on style, technique, mood and colour. Children are fascinated by digitised images particularly when they realise that they can add to, or cut out, sections to create their own unique versions.

Advantages of the computer

- It provides an opportunity to use previously acquired skills to recreate the textural effects of painting.
- Can lead to discussions on what the original artist was trying to say.
- If available, video digitiser can be used to compile a picture library. Images can then be discussed and modified using the facilities within the program.
- Many new images can be produced.

Limitations of the computer

- Colour can't always be reproduced accurately on the current range of printers.
- Computer printouts are flat compared to textured paintings.

ANOTHER WAY OF PRODUCING IMAGES: ABANDONING TRADITIONAL MATERIALS

An unusual way of using computers to create visual art is called the artificial life approach. This kind of art uses the computer to create organisms controlled by a genetic code. The artist provides the code and the rules for procreation and survival. The resulting images can be quite stunning and compare to looking at natural forms through a microscope. The most sophisticated example of this approach is derived from a branch of mathematics called fractal geometry and was developed in the seventies by Benoit Mandlebrot. (See figure C47 on page 128 in the colour section.) Fractal geometry provides scientists with a powerful tool for understanding chaos and other unpredictable patterns. For artists fractal geometry is a tool for creating realistic images of clouds, trees, lakes, mountains, landscapes and many other images. This type of technique is now frequently used by special effects designers to create environments and sets for the film industry. Who knows, perhaps it will soon be available to teachers and pupils.

5 Organisation and assessment – utilising your computer effectively

It is important for teachers to integrate the computer into the classroom effectively. It is now generally accepted that in order to develop computer skills, knowledge and understanding as well as the right attitudes towards computers, the computer needs to be readily accessible. Children should be made aware that the computer is for their use and computer activities should be part of a daily routine, not a treat for special occasions. Once this aim has been achieved we need to look at our programmes of study and identify appropriate computer programs which will offer the pupils the greatest potential for enhancing their experience.

PRACTICALITIES IN THE CLASSROOM

The computer system should be arranged on a trolley which has a four-way adaptor for connecting the various components and a circuit breaker which is fitted to the mains lead. If it is necessary to move the computer from a secure store into the classroom each day the children themselves could be involved in moving it. All the children should share this responsibility on a rotational basis: this will help to increase their confidence in handling electronic equipment. They should also take responsibility for selecting chairs to suit the height of the trolley. It might also be appropriate for the children to take responsibility for placing the computer in an appropriate position in the classroom. The sharing of these tasks helps to create a good atmosphere of co-operation.

The computer should always be positioned in such a way as to avoid reflection from windows and lighting as this will reduce the clarity of the screen image and put unnecessary strain on the children's eyes. It should also be kept away from the chalk board and sink or indeed any position which might leave it vulnerable to spillages or dust and it should be covered when not in use. Movement to and from the computer should be unhindered and you should avoid using long extension leads as these are contrary to Health and Safety Regulations. Clearly the computer also needs to be located so that it is visible to the teacher from any point in the room. There is no reason why these issues should not be discussed with the children as they form part of the learning experience. Once a suitable location has been identified a display of computer images, text or pictures could provide some useful starting points.

WORKING WITH A COMPUTER IN THE CLASSROOM

The introduction of a computer into the classroom is obviously an exciting event for all but there is the problem of having only one computer between thirty children, how do we deal with this? It is essential that all of the children should feel included. I would recommend introducing the computer or a new program to the whole class for two main reasons. Firstly, to make everybody feel involved and, secondly, because I have found that children retain much more than we might expect of such introductions and they helps to motivate them.

After the initial introduction I have found that the most effective approach is for the children to work in pairs. The pairs should contain one experienced child and one inexperienced but, of course, to decide this you need to know your children and their capabilities. All of the children should have the right to equal access on the computer. Be aware that some children may be hesitant when using the computer and they will need extra support and encouragement. A book may be placed on the computer trolley for every child to record their own experiences and achievements.

Working on the computer does not have to be an isolated activity. The paintings of the daisies in figures 12 and 12(a) on page 41 are examples of the computer being used in conjunction with a painting session. Two still lives were set up and the initial input which involved discussion about colour, shapes and spaces acted as a stimulus for both activities. The computer images are noticeably symbolic compared to the more analytic paintings.

Children enjoy looking at each others' work. An enjoyable activity is to ask the children how they created their computer pictures, what problems they encountered and how they overcame them. The discussion could involve the whole class and ideas may emerge for further development, leading on to the children making judgements about the suitability of using the computer for particular projects.

Access

Having a computer in the classroom on a permanent basis should, over a period of time, lead to a better integration of this facility into all curriculum areas. With careful organisation all children will have the opportunity to develop their skills and understanding. However, if a computer is shared between two classes or within a department, more time needs to be spent on identifying appropriate activities given that there will be less time available for each child.

SUPPORT AND ADVICE

Schools have, or are developing, policies for the integration of IT across the curriculum and have appointed co-ordinators to take responsibility for organising both resources and staff training. The school co-ordinator would be the first and most immediate source for general information and advice.

If additional specialist information is required, identify what kind of Local Education Authority (LEA) support is available. As well as an extensive inservice programme some LEAs hold computer surgeries on a regular basis where on the spot advice on particular problems can be found. (When trying to decide on a suitable program for computer art consult your art co-ordinator.) Some classroom support time may be available on a regular basis. Consider using some of this time to develop computer art alongside traditional methods.

Parents are often keen to be involved in school activities. It may be possible to involve a number of them to assist in developing computer art, particularly if they are already computer literate! However, time will need to be spent introducing them to the art programs and your teaching aims before moving into a classroom situation.

You might also consider working with your local secondary art department. This could prove useful in the sharing of ideas on computer art and could lead to some older students working with small groups of children to develop computer skills. My advice to the committed teacher is that there is no substitute for personal hands-on experience. Equip yourself with the basics outlined in figure 17 on page 47 and practice until they become second nature.

CARE AND MAINTENANCE

There are a number of basic rules which should be adhered to at all times.

> - Be aware of school policies on storage and security of equipment.
> - Keep computers away from food and drinks.
> - Keep discs in a lockable storage box.
> - Handle discs with care, keep them away from heat and any source of magnetic field such as the monitor.
> - Avoid plugging and unplugging hardware components unnecessarily as sockets can be easily damaged.
> - Use notices near the machine explaining how to look after equipment.

COPYRIGHT

When we purchase a computer program we purchase the right to use it but we do not own it. The rule is one piece of software for use on one computer. You are permitted to make one back-up or working copy of the program. It is against the law to make multiple copies of any program, if this occurs and you are found out you can be prosecuted. Remember, the rule is one machine, one program, unless:

> - the school has purchased a site licence, that is paid for permission to use the program or programs on more than one machine;
> - the LEA has purchased a Borough Licence for particular programs for use in all schools.

PRODUCING HARD COPY

The most common way to produce a hard copy of an image generated on a computer is to use a printer to output the image on to paper. You should be aware that printing is a time consuming process as each line on the screen is scanned to make the image. Therefore care should be taken when selecting images for print.

Colour printers

A colour printer is essential for printing any art as children will soon become disillusioned if their brightly coloured images can only be reproduced in black and white. Colour printers are expensive items of hardware. Needless to say, the more you pay, the better the quality of the printout. There are three types of colour printer available:

- Dot matrix – this type of printer reproduces the image from the screen as a pattern of dots. The colour is provided via a ribbon and because of this the colour may lack intensity.
- Ink jet – this kind of printer works by injecting ink on to the paper. It produces a better quality printout than the dot matrix printer.
- Laser printer – this is a high quality dot matrix printer and works in a similar way to a photocopier. Unlike the dot matrix printer the colour is provided in the form of coloured powders. Of the three types, this produces the highest quality prints and is the most expensive.

The images in this book were printed on an ink-jet printer, which is a mid-price range printer. It has some limitations in that some screen colours are not faithfully reproduced on paper but the intensity of the colour is very good. There are many different makes which are commercially available.

Printer dumps

A printer dump is a short program which allows the computer to talk to the printer and most art programs come supplied with a range of printer dumps for use with a variety of printers. Before printing, the appropriate printer driver is selected from one of the on-screen menus and once the print option is selected the printer is activated.

Print size

Print size is dictated by the capability of the printer and is usually A4 size. However, most art programs offer a choice of print sizes up to A3. Some programs offer facilities for making larger printouts. These programs have a print scaling option when a particular size is selected the computer will automatically divide the screen into a number of sections printing each in turn. These will then need to be pasted together to produce the required size.

Photographing the screen

Photographing the screen is another way in which we can produce a hard copy. To do this you need to use a camera with a manual exposure system and a shutter speed of a least one-fifteenth of a second. Faster shutter speeds will result in a line appearing across the photograph because the screen will not have been scanned properly. Likewise, you will not get a successful result if you use an automatic camera. A single lens reflex camera with a standard lens should give you good results, but you should set the camera on a tripod to avoid camera shake particularly at low shutter speeds. Normal 100 ASA print or slide film will give good results under most circumstances.

The process

- Load the camera with 100 ASA film and set it up on the tripod.
- Set the shutter speed to one-fifteenth or one-eighth of a second.
- Select the image you want to photograph and arrange the tripod in front of the computer screen.
- Adjust the position of the tripod to focus in on the image.
- Focus the camera until the screen image is clear and then set the aperture by turning the aperture ring on the lens until the needle in the viewfinder is horizontal.
- You will need to set the aperture for each picture and different screen images give off different amounts of light.
- Check that the lights in the room are off as they might be reflected on the screen. I have found that the best results are achieved by taking the photographs in a darkened room as this cuts down all reflections. The light from the computer screen is sufficient to give clear results.
- Check for any other reflections.
- Press the shutter release button.
- Keep a note of your settings for future reference.

PRESENTATION OF COMPUTER IMAGES

Once you have produced a hard copy of a computer image you will want to display it but when mounting your computer printouts for display purposes it is important to consider the following issues:

- Computer printout paper is thin and easily creases.
- Some glues soak right through computer printout paper. Avoid PVA and other water-based glues. Pritt Stick avoids creasing but is difficult to apply evenly.
- Spray mount is the best and most convenient glue that I have found. The spray gives an even coating of glue and adhesion is good. Spray mount should only be used in a well ventilated area and not by young children.
- Care in presentation will help to give a professional finish to the children's art.

Computer images can also be presented in slide show form on the computer screen. A separate program may need to be purchased for this purpose, although some art programs include such a facility. A slide show program allows you to select a number of pictures for display with a facility to control the length of time each picture stays on the screen. Such displays can be useful teaching aids to demonstrate a particular process, stimulate discussion or celebrate the work of a whole class.

EVALUATION, ASSESSMENT AND PLANNING AHEAD

Teacher evaluation

Evaluation involves looking at the value of the education which we offer and helps us to focus on our planning and performance. The purpose of this activity is that it allows teachers to reflect upon their work and the effectiveness of their teaching. This will include reflecting on whether one's aims and objectives have been achieved, as well as serving as an invaluable guide to future planning.

It may be useful as a school or department to devise a list of questions which a teacher can ask him/herself. The areas covered may include the children's level of motivation and organisation, their development in certain areas of experience, imagination and expression and the children's responses to stimuli and artefacts. It may be possible to involve the children in the teacher's evaluation by asking them some of the questions. You may ask them questions such as which programmes they enjoyed using, which programmes were most challenging and what difficulties they encountered. Evaluation must be regarded as a positive process and assessment is an important ingredient of this.

Child assessment

When we talk about assessment we mean an assessment of the quality of a child's practice and performance. There is a need to look at the qualities which are apparent and at any changes or developments which have taken place. The purpose of assessment in this context is to see what the child has achieved. You might look at the understanding and performance of a child and you should encourage the child to look at his/her approach, performance and practice and at what skills have been acquired.

The form assessment can take ranges from an informal ongoing assessment to a formal assessment involving detailed testing and grading. In computer art, or indeed any aspect of art and design, literal marking and grading should be rejected (especially with younger children) as these methods are too simplistic. We should focus on the children's response, attitude and involvement, rather than the end results.

When a child is assessed judgements will need to be made but a teacher should be sensitive to the way in which a child's art has developed. This requires experience. We need to develop informed ideas and artistic values so that we learn to recognise specific qualities in children's work. Our judgements are also affected by the context in which the art is produced. The time, the location and our values and attitudes will all influence the judgements that we make. However, a sensitive teacher should be able to judge the quality of the expression and the depth of the feeling and imagination which has gone into a pupil's work.

Assessment and record keeping may include the use of a record sheet, such as the one illustrated in figure 24 on page 87 which helps to provide a diagnosis of the stages of a child's development and ideally is kept with a few pieces of the children's work. If a portfolio of the child's art work is built-up it can illustrate the development of the child's imagery and can show the progression made in a number of areas of experience. I feel that each year, examples of some of the child's drawings should be kept to support this but there should also be work which has been done in other media including some computer work. The pieces of work become more interesting if some of them are accompanied by a short piece of writing either by the child or teacher (depending on the ability of the child) which describes the context of the work, any future development and their feelings about the work. Such a portfolio is evidence of a child's creative progress but also serves as an illuminating and interesting personal document.

Planning ahead

The ability to respond to the needs of children is the hallmark of a good teacher. In art and design we must allow for both the spontaneous activities which occur naturally in any classroom situation as well as the more structured activities which are an essential part of any developmental approach. Figure 25 on page 88 outlines a broad and developmental art programme which is linked with IT capability and suggestions for computer art activities. The activities listed are not exhaustive but suggest starting points for development.

WHERE NEXT?

In real terms computer development in the visual arts is way behind the major changes already taking place in the musical arts where computers are a major driving force allowing sounds to be created and modified electronically without loss of quality. There is, however, no doubt that the computer has transformed working methods in the printing, publishing, textile, fashion, advertising and design industries. It saves time, it is very accurate and gives designers the chance to manipulate images on screen, without the danger of spoiling the original. Images can also be stored for reference, providing a useful record of the way in which a particular design progressed. Being able to produce a wide range of sample colour and typeface layouts and being able to scale easily, designers can make informed decisions quickly.

Sample term record sheet   Name: [illegible]isha Patel   Age 7   Computer art experience

Term Autumn	Investigating and making	Knowledge and understanding	IT capability	Experience and achievements
Topic Water	Looked at pattern and colour Observational drawings ↓ three computer images ↓ developed into a fabric collage	Responded to artists' interpretations of water Discussed colour, shape and pattern Showed ability to discuss feelings about content and mood Liked work of Monet and Hockney	She is able to retrieve an image but needs help when saving	Demonstrated confidence in controlling the mouse and selecting tools from the screen Was able to work collaboratively She was able to select from a range of media when deciding how to develop the computer image

Figure 24 Sample record sheet

	Investigating and making	Knowledge and understanding	IT capability	Art development	Art and the computer
By the age of 5	• Explore and experiment with a wide range of materials both 2 and 3D, based on their own experience	• Talk about their environment at home and school. Talk about and handle objects (made and natural) sort objects and look at interesting features. Use of stimulating picture books • Look at works of art and look at story pictures and pattern pictures	• Attitudes, home, equal opportunities, encourage both boys and girls. Positive role models. Setting easy challenges using a variety of programmes. Fun, delight, sense of achievement and sense of control for the individual. Discuss use of computer in everyday life	• Abstract scribble • Wide use of media and material. Some representation of symbols emerging • Build up symbols often alongside scribble', experience and experiment • Figures, self, houses, trees, animals, etc • Simple forms and constructions are sometimes named. Pleasure of colour, pattern and form in their own right • Personal value regarding scale • Shapes are seldom overlapped • Role play with 2 and 3D work e.g. puppets, masks and figures	• Scribble/non-figurative paintings, drawing, and printing • Experimenting with using colour • Pattern/shape • Overlapping shapes • Individual attempts at symbolic images
By the age of 7	• Record observations from direct experiences of natural and made environments • Respond to memory and imagination • Collect images and objects to stimulate and inform their own work • Explore a range of materials, tools and techniques • Explore how images can be used through line and tone, working with a variety of tools and materials • Explore mixing from primary colours • Explore and recreate pattern and texture in natural and made forms • Explore the use of shape, form and space in making images and artefacts • Make 3D work for a variety of purposes • Review their work and modify it as they see the need for change • Talk about their work	• Identify examples of art in school environment • Recognise different kinds of art by sculptors, painters, printmakers etc • Make broad distinctions between the elements of art, colour, shape, form, tone, texture and pattern • Talk about and respond to the work of influential artist from a variety of styles, times and cultures • Recognise the difference between present and past artists' work • Respond practically to the content, theme or mood of a work of art • Begin to make connections between their own and other artists' work	• Select items from a computer screen • Use computer pictures to convey meaning • Able to use a keyboard, mouse, touch screen, other input devices with different software • Retrieve saved pictures • Able to use computer generated pictures and symbols to communicate meaning • Realise that the computer can be used for tasks that can also be accomplished by other means • Use IT for storage and retrieval of information	• Need for selected detail • Imagery developing into a means for expression and communicating ideas, events, imaginings and stories • Growing desire to analyse and to make likenesses • Enjoyment in pattern, colour, texture and form • For some children a need for visual realism	• Confidence in experimentation • Enjoyment and exploration of pattern • Use of the computer as a starting point for each area of experience as appropriate • Ability to use the computer to communicate ideas • Ability to adapt and change images
By the age of 11	• Select and record images from firsthand observation • Respond to memory and imagination using a range of media • Use a sketch-book to record observations and ideas • Experiment with ideas from different source materials, tools and techniques and explain how they have used them to develop their work • Apply their knowledge and experience to different materials, tools and techniques using them experimentally and expressively • Experiment with different quantities of line and tone in making images • Apply the principles of colour mixing in making various kinds of images • Experiment with pattern and texture in designing and making images and artefacts • Experiment with ways of representing shape, form and space • Plan and make 3D structures using various materials and for different purposes • Adapt and modify their work • Use specialist terms	• Recognise that there are different kinds of art made for different purposes • Understand and use subject specific terms such as landscape, still life, mural, design, 3D, craft, making broad distinctions within the elements of art and design • Understand how the work of artists is influenced by time and place • Recognise the characteristics of art from different periods, styles and genres, Classical, Renaissance, Impressionism, Pop and identify influential artists • Understand some of the methods and materials that artists use • Describe and make comparisons between their own work and that of other artists • Experiment with some of the methods and approaches used by other artists, and use these imaginatively to inform their own work	• Create a drawing on the computer screen and modify it • To use a drawing program to create an image and save it to disc • Produce computer images to present information e.g. to draw and paint • To combine text and image (desktop publishing) • Create a motif for repeat pattern • Amend a drawing to illustrate different colours or pattern	• Use of symbolism and analysis • Interest in dramatic events and the environment • Fascination with detail and selections of things as well as whole views • Narrative drawings and paintings • Interest in designing, making models • Recording, analysing • Expressing and communicating • Interest in scale/proportion and spatial qualities • Experience in handling media, materials and tools	• Use the computer as a starting point for an idea • Use the computer as part of a process • Computer image as end-product • Ability to use the zoom facility for detailed work • Produce a repeat pattern for design work • Ability to save stages in the development of an image and to make choices • Ability to use the computer as an expressive tool • 3D, receding colours and perspective, recognise when the computer is an appropriate tool

Figure 25 Planning for progression and continuity in art and Information Technology

Fashion and textile designers use Computer Aided Design (CAD) to produce variations on repeats and colourways on screen, so that they can see what a design looks like before committing it to cloth. Set designers, product designers and interior designers use it to visualise spatial relationships before embarking on full scale production. Architects create plans for buildings using CAD, which they can then look at from all angles.

In relation to fine art there is still a degree of scepticism about computer imagery which is not unlike the arguments which surrounded the recognition of photography as a visual art form. This scepticism has been reinforced by the fact that the creation of computer images has been limited by the resolution on most computer screens and the lack of suitable output devices.

As we move through the nineties I would anticipate an increase in the use of computers for art as more individuals begin to realise their potential and their ability to create quality images which are comparable to other art media. Clearly artists would not be interested in using computers if versions of the traditional tools were not available but, with technological improvements in display technology and image processing techniques, artists in the future will be able to imitate the effects of oil paint, pastels, and charcoal whilst at the same time taking advantage of more advanced ways of manipulating images.

In primary schools a basic art program has the potential to be used in many different ways and therefore we should not worry too much about keeping up with new developments in both hardware and software as these are constantly changing. It is the skills and attitudes which are learnt during the process of teaching computer art which are important as these are transferable to other computer systems. Above all it is our imagination, enthusiasm and motivation which should be the driving force behind creative expression and not the computer or programs which we use. The teachers I have worked with had little or no experience of using the computer for art activities but as their confidence increased they were willing to explore more advanced facilities as the need for them arose.

For those individuals who wish to add to their basic systems I would recommend either a scanner or digitiser as an alternative input device. The former allows children's drawings and photographs to be loaded from paper originals on to the computer and a digitiser enables frames or pictures to be transferred from either a video camera or recorder. These images can then be worked on using paint software. (See figure C48 on page 128 in the colour section.)

A useful software addition would be a desktop publishing program. This can be used to extend the graphic work done by children by allowing images produced with paint programs, scanners and digitisers to be combined with text to produce newsletters, posters, illustrated stories and poems.

In the nineteenth century the impressionist painters were quick to exploit technical developments within their own craft. It was the freedom offered by being able to purchase tubes of ready mixed oil paint and ready made canvases that opened-up many possibilities for them. Amongst these was the ability to work easily outside. These days, as children develop their skills and confidence in using art programs, they will begin to evolve a style which has its foundation in the imitation of traditional media but with the potential to explore many new possibilities. Picasso once said that art does not evolve by itself but that people's ideas change and therefore art also changes in order to express those ideas. What better justification could there be for exploring the use of computers in art and design?

Glossary of terms

BYTE	A unit of computer memory
CAA	Computer Aided Art
CAD	Computer Aided Design
CAL	Computer Assisted Learning
Cursor	The floating pointer on the screen referred to in this text as a pointer
Cut and paste	The ability to cut out an area of the screen and move it to another place
Data	Information stored on a computer disc
Default	The computer setting when it comes from the factory or when a preference hasn't been specified by the user for a particular option. The settings can be changed by the user. This may be necessary with certain software
Desktop	The first screen to appear when the computer is switched on. Usually a blank screen with a disc drive icon and a number of pull-down or pop-up menus
Desktop publishing	Sophisticated software which facilitates the combination of text and images in newspaper type format
Digitise	To take a picture with a video camera connected to a computer. The pictures can be worked on with the appropriate software
Disc drive	The part of the hardware which takes the discs
Dithered colour	The term applied to the making of mixed coloured brushes
DOS	Disc Operating System – this is the means by which the computer manages and organises information

File name	The name given to a particular image when saved
Floppy disc	Like the folders in a filing cabinet – used to store information
Format	Discs must be formatted before information can be recorded. Discs formatted on one computer system cannot be used on others unless they share the same operating system or DOS
Graphics tablet	An input device which looks like a small drawing board with an attached pen or stylus
Hands on	Working on a computer
Hard copy	Printed paper image from the computer screen
Hard disc	An internal disc drive of high capacity. Hard disc machines are usually more expensive but are able to hold information when the machine is switched off. Software can be loaded on to the hard disc, thus eliminating the need to load the software from floppy disc when the computer is switched on
Hardware	The term used to describe all the components of a computer system. Monitor, keyboard, processor, printer, mouse etc.
Icon	A symbol used to describe options on screen
Initialise	Similar to format, preparing a disc ready to store information
IT	Information Technology
Joystick	An input device used to control the cursor on the screen

Megabyte	Approximately 1,000,000 bytes. Some software will not run on computers with less than one megabyte of memory
Menu	A list of choices displayed on the screen which can be selected by directing the pointer and clicking the mouse button
Monitor	The computer screen
Mouse	A hand-held object with up to three buttons. The roller-bearing mechanism on its base allows it to be moved across the desktop. See pointer
Operating system	The program which controls the functions and operations of the computer
Peripheral	Any equipment which can be attached to a computer such as the mouse, joystick, printer etc.
Pixel	Picture element which describes the dots on the computer screen
Pointer	Usually an arrow which is displayed on screen – it moves when the mouse is moved
Printer	A piece of hardware which is used to gain a hard copy from the computer screen
Dot-matrix printer	The term used to describe a printer which produces images as a series of dots
Ink-jet printer	The term used to describe a printer which injects ink on to the paper to create the image
Laser printer	A dot-matrix printer which produces high quality printouts
Printer driver	A short program used to give the computer instructions for a particular printer

Prompt	A screen message which appears when a computer is waiting for instructions
Resolution	A term used to describe the quality of the screen image. High resolution equals a fine or finer image. Low or medium equals a coarser image
Scaling	The term used to describe how the screen image can be increased or decreased in size for printing
Scanner	An input device which enables text or graphic images from paper originals to be loaded into the computer
Screen dump	The term used to describe the transfer of the screen image to paper
Software	A program which gives the computer a particular set of instructions
Touchscreen	A special screen which allows the user to select items by touching the appropriate screen icon
UNDO	A program facility which allows the last marks created to be erased.
User friendly	The term used to describe how easy the hardware or software is to use
VDU	Visual Display Unit which is the same thing as a screen or monitor
Video digitiser	Hardware which turns signals from a video camera or recorder into digital form for use within certain types of software
Wimps	Windows, Icons, Menus and Pointers
Window	A particular screen
WYSIWIG	What You See Is What You Get: that is, the screen image is the same size as the printout
Zoom	A software facility which enables a selected area of the screen to be enlarged for editing. The image is changed by altering each pixel

Bibliography

Bernstein, Saul and McGarry, Leo. *Making Art on Your Computer*, Watson–Guptoll Publications, New York, USA, 1986

Morgan, Margaret. *Art 4–11*, Basil Blackwell, Oxford, 1988

Cooper, Michael. *Electronic 'Paint'*, National Council For Educational Technology (NCET), London, 1990

Scott, Joan. (Ed.) *Computergraphia*, Gulf Publishing Company, Houston, USA, 1984

Barnes, Rob. *Teaching Art to Young Children 4–9*, Unwin Hyman, London, 1987

Barnes, Rob. *Art, Design and Topic work 8–13*, Unwin Hyman, London, 1989

Clement, Robert. *The Art Teacher's Handbook*, Hutchinson, London, 1986

HMI. *The Teaching and Learning of Information Technology*, HMSO, London, 1991

Kurzweil, Raymond. *The Age of Intelligent Machines*, Massachusetts Institute of Technology, Massachusetts, (MIT) USA, 1990

Palfreman, Jon and Swade, Doron. *The Dream Machine*, BBC Publications, London, 1991

Wise, David. *Design in focus*, Wayland (Publishers Ltd), Brighton, 1990

Cooper, Michael. (Ed.) *Developing Criteria for Art and Design Software*, Homerton College, Cambridge, 1991

HMI. *Information Technology and Special Education Needs in School*: a review by HMI, HMSO, London, 1990

National Council for Educational Technology. *Focus on I.T.,* National Council for Educational Technology (NCET) Coventry, 1990

Govier, Heather. *I.T. in the Primary School*, Micro-Electronics Education Support Unit, (MESU), Coventry, 1989

Ellis, Judith. *Equal Opportunities and Computer Education in the Primary School*, Equal Opportunities Commission and MESU, Coventry, 1988

Hughes, Robert. *The Shock of the New*, BBC Publications, London, 1980

HMSO. *Art in the National Curriculum*, HMSO, London, 1992

HMSO. *Information Technology in the National Curriculum*, HMSO, London, 1990

Lincoln, W.L.R., and Maddocks, D.H. *Information Technology a Curriculum Map*, Hunter Press, 1990

Colour section – computer art from four to eleven years

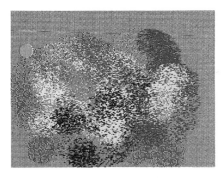

Figure C1   Airbrush effect

Figure C2   Colour palette

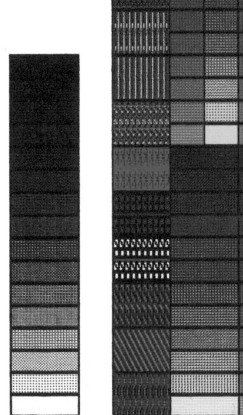 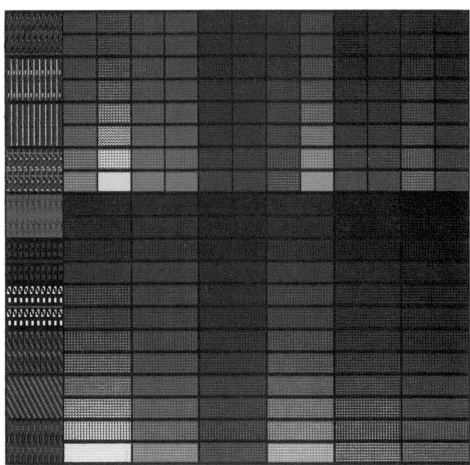

Children's art and the computer

Figure C3   Cut and paste

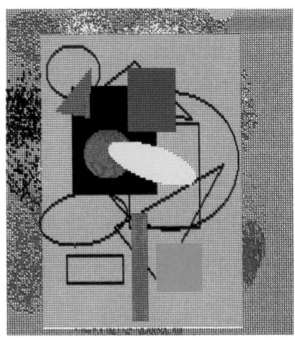

Figure C4   Geometric shape

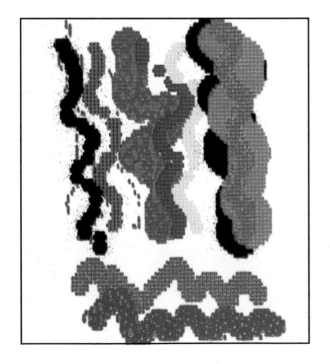

Figure C5   Line drawing tools

Figure C6   Painting tools

Figure C7   Fill function

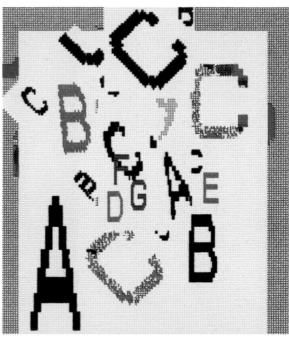

Figure C8   Text. This picture was produced as the result of Challenge 8 – text (see page 51)

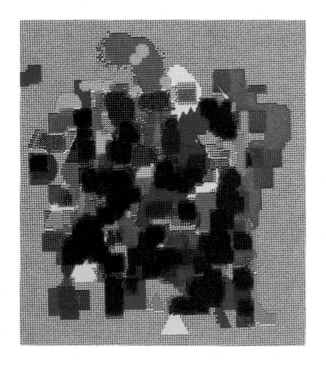

Figure C9   Watercolour or wash

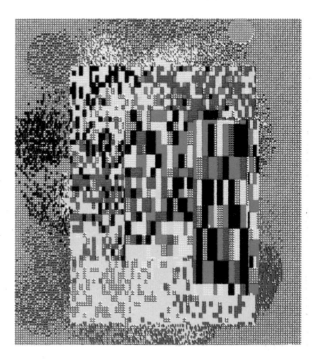

Figure C10   Zoom

Figures C11–13
Fairground series
showing the effect of
different sized pixels
on the final printed
image, by two eight-year-
old girls

Figure C11

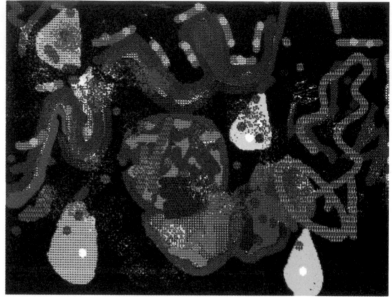

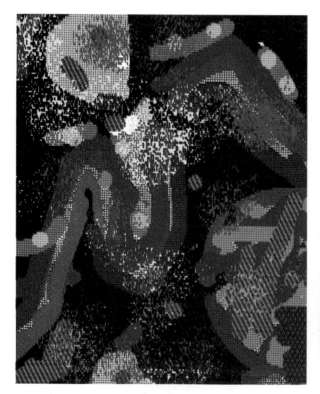

Figure C12 *Fairground series*

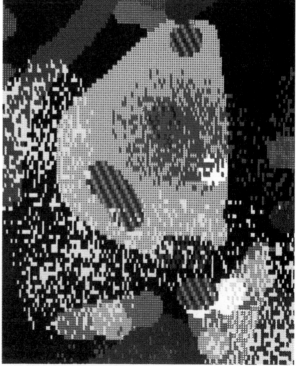

Figure C13 *Fairground series*

100

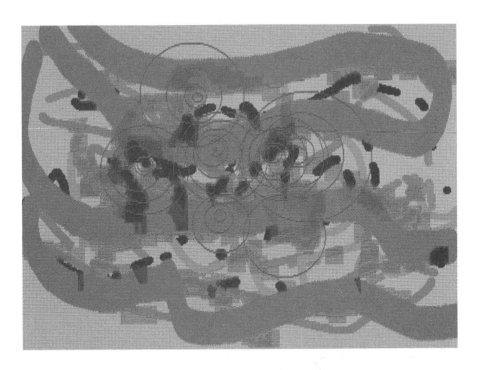

Figure C14 *Water series* to show the effect that paper quality has on an image, by a seven-year-old boy

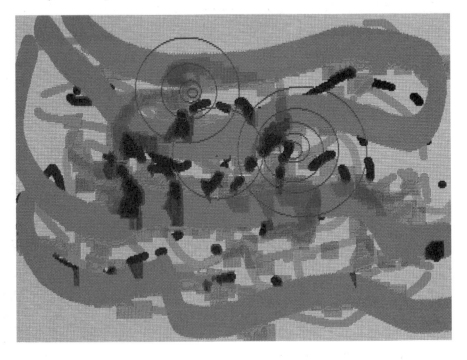

Figure C15 *Water series*

Figures C16–19
Fairground series by
two eight-year-old girls,
showing the effect that
putting different
substrates through the
printer has on the image.

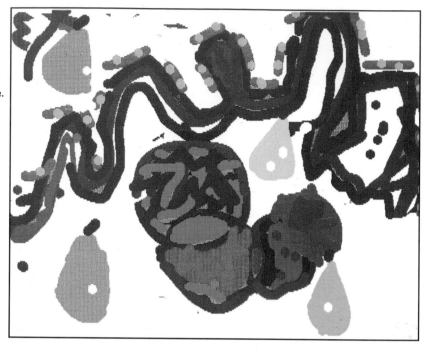

Figure C16 is reproduced on computer paper

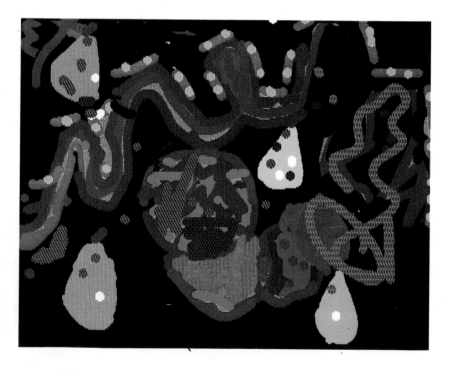

Figure C17 is reproduced on cartridge paper

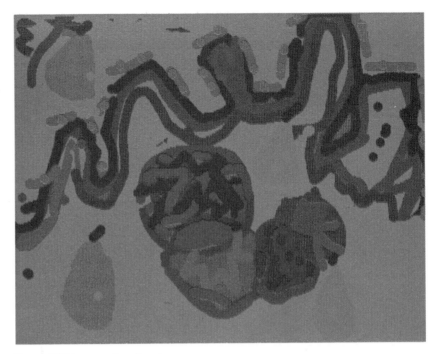

Figure C18 is reproduced on Ingres paper

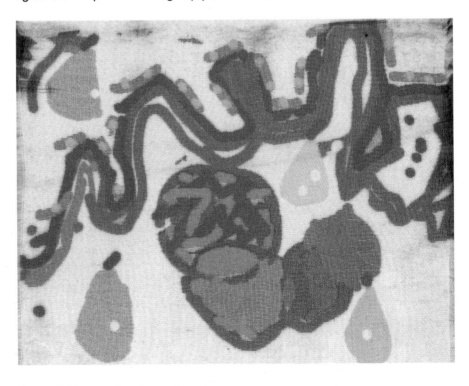

Figure C19 is reproduced on a piece of cotton

103

Figure C20   Exploration of paint tools and colour showing a dotted line effect caused by rapid movement of the mouse. This picture was produced as the result of Challenge 1 – mark-making, by a four-year-old girl. (see page 48)

Figure C21 *My shoe.*
This illustration shows
the stepped appearance
of curves caused by the
pixel make-up of the
screen, by an eight-year-
old boy

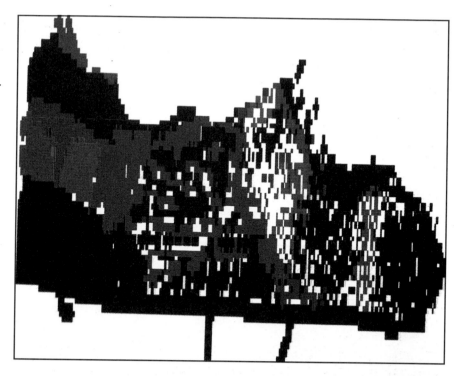

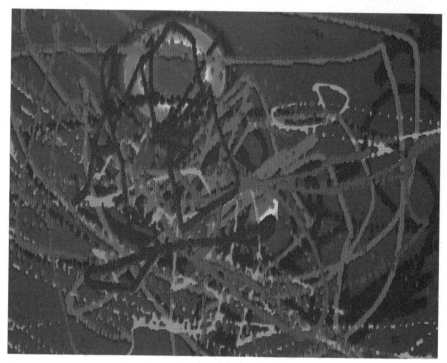

Figure C22 *Free exploration*, by a four-year-old boy

Figure C23   Challenge 2 – geometric shapes, by a five-year-old boy (see page 49)

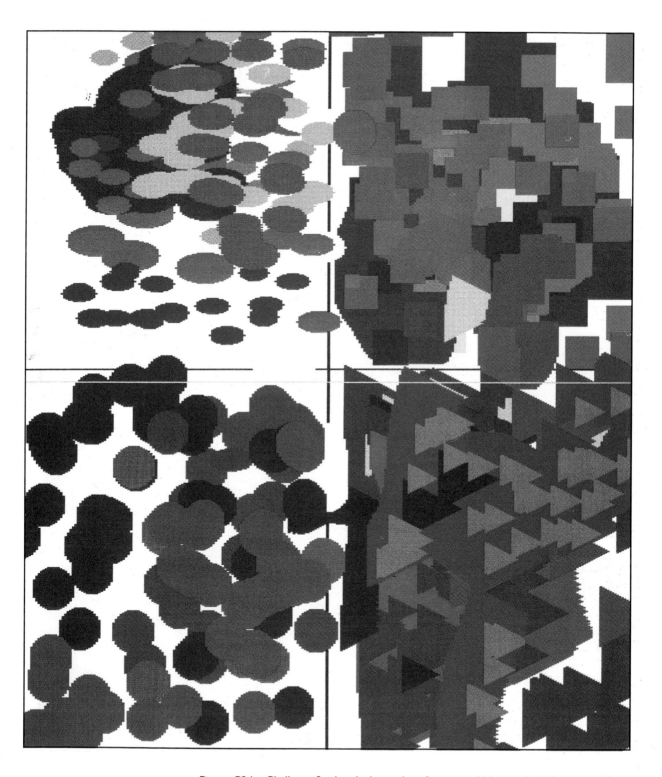

Figure C24   Challenge 3 – brush shapes, by a five-year-old boy and girl (see page 49)

Figure C25   Challenge 4 – watercolour or wash, by a seven-year-old girl (see page 49)

Figure C26   Challenge 5 – airbrush landscape after looking at paintings by Monet, by a seven-year-old girl (see page 50)

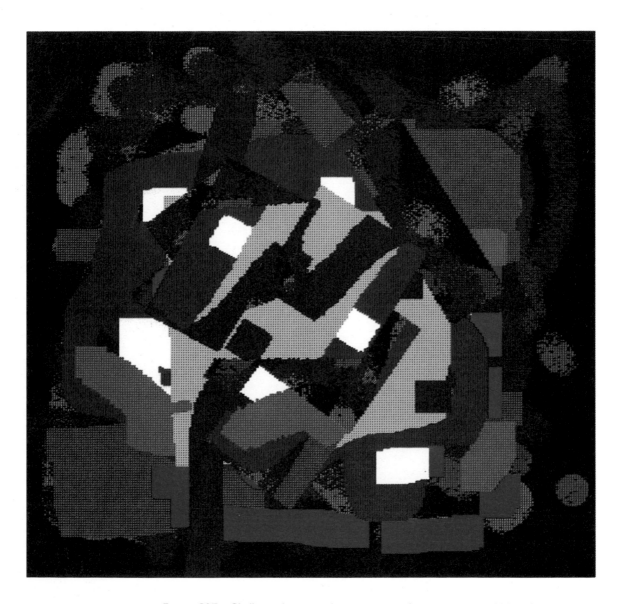

Figure C27   Challenge 6 – cut and paste or copy, by a seven-year-old boy (see page 50)

Figure C28

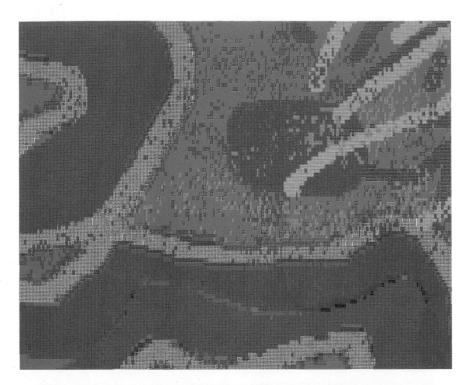

Figure C28(a)

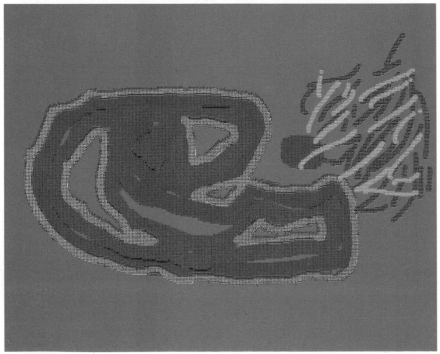

Figures C28 and C28(a)   Challenge 7 – zoom or enlarge, by a seven-year-old girl (see page 51)

Figure C29

Figure C29(a)

Figures C29 and C29(a)   *Winter* from a project on seasons. The computer was used as a starting point for a painting, by a seven-year-old boy

Figure C30

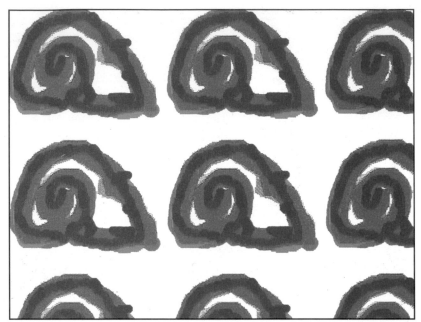

Figures C30 and C30(a)
Shell series using the
computer as part of a
process culminating in a
print on fabric, by a
seven-year-old boy

Figure C30(a)

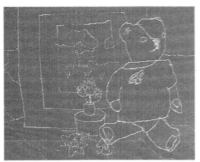

Figure C31

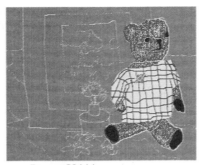

Figure C31(a)

Figure C31(b)

Figure C31(c)

Figures C31 and C31(a, b) *Still life with teddy bear*. The three pictures in a strip show
the stages leading up to the final image in C31(c), by an eleven-year-old girl

Figure C32   *Still life of dried flowers*, by an eleven-year-old girl

Figures C33 and C33(a)
Basil in oil pastels and
as a computer image, by
a six-year-old girl

Figure C33

Figure C33(a)

Figure C34

Figures C34, C34(a, b, c, d)   A pastel drawing and four computer images showing how an image can be translated from one medium to another. Note how the artist has used cut and paste to move the car. The artist was delighted to find that the fragments of image left behind looked like a reflection. By a seven-year-old boy

Figure C34(a)

Figure C34(b)

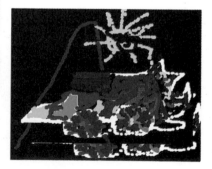

Figure C34(c)

Figure C34(d)   The finished image

Figure C35   *After Van Gogh*, by an eight-year-old boy

Figure C36   This image, which is based on a Matisse cut out, shows how the same shape is affected by different coloured backgrounds, by an eight-year-old boy and girl

Figure C37 Colours can be used to create mood, by an eleven-year-old boy

Figure C38 Creating multiple images on screen, by a seven-year-old girl

Figure C39

Figures C39 and C39(a)
A collage inspired by a
section of a computer
painting of a snowman,
by an eight-year-old boy

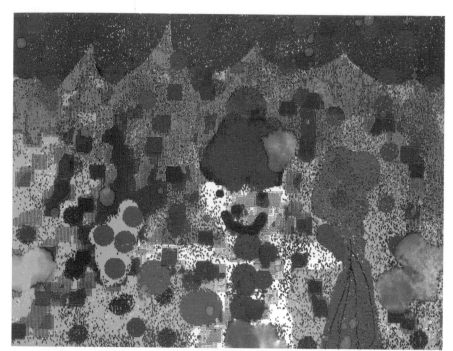

Figure C39(a)

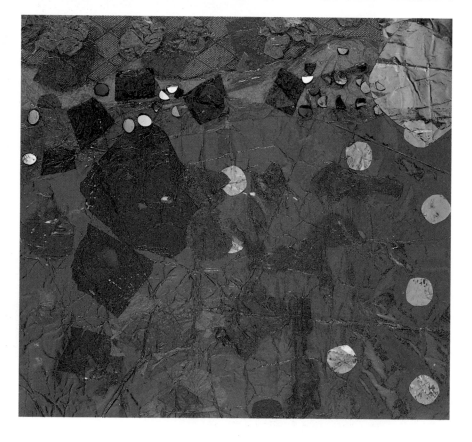

Figure C40

Figure C40(a)

Figure C40(c)

Figure C40(b)

Figures C40 and C40(a, b, c)   A computer project on shape and pattern which began with computer images (the triangle C40 and the circle C40(a)) which were then cut and collaged and finally worked on using paint, by boys and girls aged seven to eleven years

Figure C41

Figure C41(b)

Figure C41(a)

Figures C41 and C41(a, b, c, d, e)   Computer interpretations of water. C41(b) was translated into weave C41(d), and C41(c) was translated into a fabric print using a string block and sprayed with different coloured inks, by eight-year-old boys and girls

Figure C41(d)

Figure C41(c)

Figure C41(e)

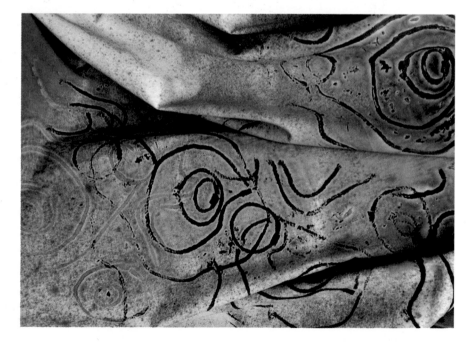

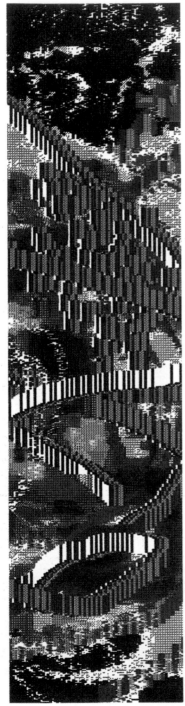

Figure C42   Figure C42(a)

Figures C42 and C42(a)   Three-dimensional effect created by using a dithered brush,
by a ten-year-old boy

Figure C43(a)   The image coloured in using the fill tool, by a ten-year-old boy

Figure C43   The image on the left shows the original design which was transferred to the screen on an acetate sheet. The image on the right is the outline image on the computer screen, by a ten-year-old boy

Figure C43(b)   The logo has been repeated using the cut and paste facility

Figure C43(c)   The same repeat image with the letter outlines filled in using the design as the fill

125

Figure C44   Individual logos assembled to create a large wall hanging

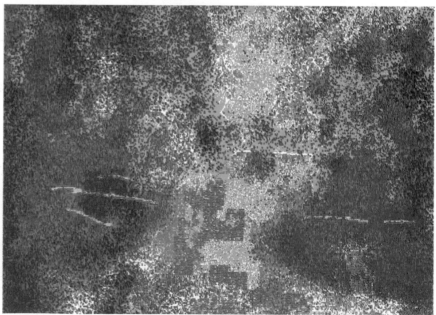

Figure C45   Interpretation of a Monet painting, by a seven-year-old girl

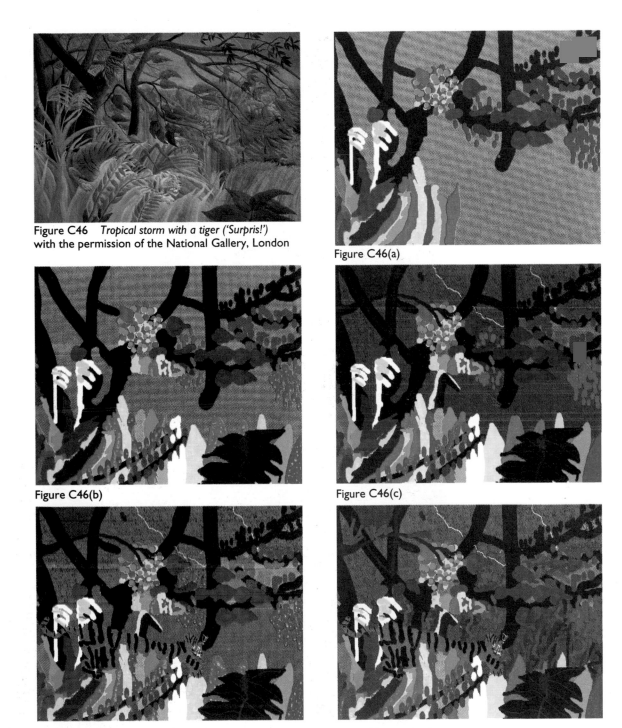

Figure C46   *Tropical storm with a tiger ('Surpris!')* with the permission of the National Gallery, London

Figure C46(a)

Figure C46(b)

Figure C46(c)

Figure C46(d)

Figure C46(e)

Figure C46(a, b, c, d, e)   A sequence showing the development of a computer image using Rousseau's painting as a starting point, by an eight-year-old girl

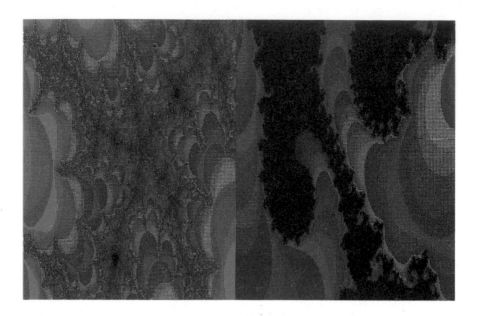

Figure C47   A Benoit Mandlebrot image based on fractal geometry

Figure C48   Digitised image of *The Japanese Bridge* Monet's garden, Giverny, France